Tony Greig: My Story

TONY GREIG
with Alan Lee

My Story

Stanley Paul
London Melbourne Sydney Auckland Johannesburg

Stanley Paul & Co. Ltd

An imprint of the Hutchinson Publishing Group

3 Fitzroy Square, London WIP 6JD

Hutchinson Group (Australia) Pty Ltd
30–32 Cremorne Street, Richmond South, Victoria 3121
PO Box 151, Broadway, New South Wales 2007

Hutchinson Group (NZ) Ltd
32–34 View Road, PO Box 40–086, Glenfield, Auckland 10

Hutchinson Group (SA) (Pty) Ltd
PO Box 337, Bergvlei 2012, South Africa

First published 1980

© Tony Greig 1980

Set in Intertype Baskerville

Printed in Great Britain by The Anchor Press Ltd
and bound by Wm Brendon & Son Ltd
both of Tiptree, Essex

ISBN 0 09 133370 9

The author and publishers would like to thank the
following for permission to reproduce copyright
photographs: J. B. Arseniou, Central Press Photos
Limited, The *Daily Express*, Patrick Eagar, the *Leicester
Mercury*, Scope Features, the *Sun* and Syndication
International Limited.

to Donna, Samantha, Mark, Mum and Dad

Contents

1   Epilepsy   9

2   Childhood   20

3   The family   30

4   Schooldays   40

5   Working a passage   50

6   Sussex   63

7   Donna   74

8   South Africa   81

9   Early Tests   91

10   Tours and traumas   103

11   England, my England!   115

12   A week in the life   129

13   Goodbye to all that?   148

14   Packing up   157

15   Packer and beyond   167

     Career record   177

     Index   183

Editor's Note

This book is based on tape-recordings of discussions between Tony Greig and myself or taken from transcripts provided by him. These I have merely edited. The sections in italic type are my own comments.

Alan Lee

I

Epilepsy

Great sportsmen the world over have a story to tell. Sometimes their success has been achieved only after overcoming an environmental disadvantage or physical handicap. Some, naturally, have been luckier than others, but relatively few can look back upon a completely comfortable path to fame.

It is safe to state, however, that the story of Anthony William Greig ranks among the more extraordinary in the history of professional sport. His nationality, background and volatile personality should all logically have conspired against his rise to the pinnacle of world cricket.

Much of this is known. Yet the overwhelming obstacle in his chosen career remained a public secret for more than twenty years. Tony Greig, who had captained county and country before leading the world's players in the most controversial revolution cricket has known, is an epileptic.

We were in the fifth and final set when it happened. Charlie Pope and I, old mates yet regular rivals on the tennis court.

Charlie was at Dale College, 100 miles south of my native Queenstown and the traditional local rivals of my own school, Queen's College. Time and again we found ourselves in opposition when our schools met in the annual tennis 'derby' match.

We were both 14 when the big day came around again and, once more, we were drawn against each other in the singles tournament. Charlie had taken the first set, I had won the next two and he had saved the match with the fourth.

As we began the last set I started suffering from an unpleasant giddy feeling, something I found impossible to explain. I felt confused and a little bewildered, yet the words of my mother somehow reassured me. For months she had vainly protested that I was trying to do too much sport. I remember she had gone so far as to visit our school headmaster and ask whether it was necessary for me to spend every afternoon and every evening of my life practising cricket, tennis and rugby.

Up to now I had ignored her warnings and gone on with my exhausting routine. School began at 7.30 a.m. every weekday and was over before two o'clock. I needed no more than a few minutes to change into tennis kit and the next two hours were spent on the court before a second quick change in time for rugby practice at 4.30 p.m.

Every winter night I would get home with darkness falling, invariably whacked but ready for nothing more than supper, the compulsory hour's homework, and bed. That was my life and I wanted it to stay that way, yet, as dizziness began to overtake me during the fifth set against Charlie Pope on that summer Saturday afternoon in Queenstown, I wondered whether Mum had been right all along and I was overdoing things.

Bad as I felt, though, throwing in the towel never entered my head. With typical schoolboy blinkers on, I was obsessed with somehow soldiering through, winning that final set and helping my school defeat the old enemy.

It wasn't to be. All I remember of the awful moment is walking back to serve, throwing up the ball . . . then darkness.

Later, I learned that my doubles partner, Bob McKenzie, had been the first to reach me. His parents were both at the match and it was they who drove me home at the outset of the most shattering period of my life.

At first I hadn't a clue what was wrong with me. Neither had my parents. The first indication I was given of the seriousness of the condition came from a man who had acted as our family doctor for years past.

His name was Sandy Voortman and I trusted him completely. He had brought us all into the world – my two sisters, my little brother and myself – and had always been on hand whenever anything went wrong. Now, suddenly, we needed him as never before.

Dr Voortman had himself been an accomplished athlete, and his involvement in sport gave me a greater respect for him and, I believe, helped him to communicate with me on a possible explanation.

Naturally, he was apprehensive about committing himself on such a far-reaching issue and his advice was sound. Go to Cape Town, he said, and get an expert opinion from the Groote Schuur Hospital – the place where, later, Christiaan Barnard first made himself and his transplants famous.

By now I needed no telling that this was a situation which could affect the rest of my life. The next step was obviously critical and, under any other circumstances, it would have been a memorable excursion.

Here I was, a 14-year-old country boy, travelling hundreds of miles to a city that was tantamount to a new world. But I could feel no sense of excitement or anticipation, only a dread that my life could soon be crashing about me due to a condition I simply could not understand.

Our appointment was with a specialist called Gonski, then apparently one of South Africa's leading authorities on neurology and now practising in Australia. To a small boy like me, the office block where our meeting was arranged appeared as a huge sky-scraper. Thinking back now, I shouldn't think it had more than six or seven storeys, but Queenstown just didn't have buildings like that.

The first thing Mr Gonski did was test my reflexes. He reported that they were excellent and that verdict illogically filled me with relief. Naïve optimism convinced me that this was proof enough to dispel everyone's silly fears.

It was decided, however, to go ahead with a series of tests, and at the end of the session I remember Mr Gonski telling my parents that I was suffering from a mild and common form of epilepsy that would probably go away.

It never did go away, and now it never will. Since then, I have educated myself to control the onset of the condition by the simplest possible method . . . sleep. At that stage, however, the only thought in my head was the lingering doubt that this was an illness which could alienate me from the sporting world I loved. I still didn't understand it, and I don't think I had ever heard of epilepsy, but I had gathered enough to know that it was not a trivial complaint.

Mr Gonski prescribed certain drugs, later to have an effect not without its humorous consequences. Years afterwards, when I was higher in the senior school, my maths teacher gave me a roasting in class and then went to my parents to plead with them to stop me smoking.

Smoking was completely taboo for any of the pupils at our school. Six strokes with the cane was the instant punishment for a first offence; expulsion could follow if you were caught again. Drinking, whether in school or holiday time, was considered an even more violent breach and, for that, expulsion was immediate.

This master believed that my lethargic behaviour in class was due to the influence of cigarettes – an obvious assumption as he had no way of telling that I was, to all intents and purposes, on drugs.

I had never had a cigarette in my life and the well-meaning teacher, a close friend of my parents who wished me no harm, probably felt a good deal of surprise and embarrassment when he was told the real reason for my lethargy.

Throughout the years between discovery of the condition and the end of my schooldays, I shied away from any conversation on the subject. I accepted that I had to live with this problem, but it made it no easier for me to discuss it.

My family's reaction was primarily one of protection. They needed to remind me every day of the year, by way of ensuring I took the tablets. Doctors constantly stressed to them how vitally important it was that I kept to the prescribed dose and, by drumming this into me morning and night, they were only doing their best for my safety and future. Yet I hated every single reminder.

My distress was most acute when relatives or friends came to the house and my parents had to answer questions on my condition. That was something I could not handle, and many were the times that I got up and fled from the room.

Whenever I had an attack I felt I was over-protected – something else that both puzzled and amazed me. Dr Voortman generally gave me an injection that would put me out for a complete day and night. When I came round again, there would, in my young mind, be absolutely nothing wrong with me. Yet, on occasions, I was kept in bed for as long as a week.

If, at that stage, I had not yet learned exactly how I should cope with an impending attack, I was at least capable of recognizing the symptoms and accepting the inevitable. It was a gradual build-up and the interval between attacks was sometimes as long as a year or two years. Then I would get dizzy, pass out, sleep for twenty-four hours and feel ready to resume life as if nothing had happened, only to be told that I had to stay in bed. For my young and active mind, this was an intolerable situation.

I longed to be told that this was nothing that would interfere with my cricket, my tennis and my rugby. But nobody could give me any such assurance.

Instead, I was told that I was not allowed to do a whole range of things because of the danger involved. I was to stop riding a bicycle. If I wanted to swim I would have to be consistently in adult company. There was to be no playing or walking near the edge of a cliff.

Here I drew the line. OK, so I had a dangerous illness. But my life had to go on, and I intended to live it the way I wanted. I went on riding my bicycle where and when I chose. I swam whenever I felt like it, often alone. And I refused to make any conscious effort to avoid high places.

Maybe I was foolhardy, a stubborn martyr. But I was lucky. I came to no harm by carrying on just the way I had always done. I never had an attack while on a bike, I never passed out while swimming, and gradually my family realized that they would take half my life away if they insisted on chaining me with safety regulations. So they let me do things my way, possibly reluctantly, possibly fearfully – but, thankfully, without disastrous consequences.

Only once did an attack cause me any physical damage. I think it was only the second time I had passed out and it happened in the pantry of our Queenstown home.

My mother often used to bake delicious biscuits and put them under the care of our cook, Sophie.

To get to the biscuits, however, I needed a high stool. It was on that, reaching up to the highest shelf in the pantry for my nightly goodies, that dizziness attacked me one night with painful results.

I was found lying on the floor of the pantry, with a black eye, chipped teeth and an assortment of bruises. By far the most serious wound, however, was the one to my pride caused by the inevitable discovery of my biscuit burglaries.

Then, as on almost every other black-out occasion during my time in South Africa, I was put into a deep and prolonged sleep by the needle of Dr Voortman. That needle, and whatever its contents may have been, provided relief, drained away the effects of the attack and left me feeling fit and refreshed. Yet, since going to England, I have found no one willing to administer similar treatment.

Epilepsy is incurable; it can be controlled but never eliminated. Yet I have to say that I have no real faith in the medical profession when it comes to such complex neurology. I have simply formulated my own pattern of treatment which revolves around sleeping whenever I start to feel giddy.

It has led to some embarrassing situations when I have walked out of meetings and left bars and parties without a word of explanation. But to me it is absolutely essential.

I am the sort of person who can generally sleep anywhere, and at any time of day. Whenever possible, I like to have a nap during the afternoon, and even during matches I often stretch out on a couch or even on the floor of the dressing-room, sometimes when I am only one wicket away from going out to bat.

Dropping off to sleep then is no problem at all. But, as soon as I get the tell-tale dizzy feeling, sleep is impossible without the help of a couple of knock-out tablets.

Over the years it has become increasingly apparent to me that I am far more vulnerable to an attack when I'm bored. If I keep active, I am generally in little danger. This theory holds good for all but a couple of instances – my very first attack, on the tennis court, and one I was to have ten years later on the opening day of my début for Eastern Province.

It was the season of 1970–1 and I had arrived back in South Africa after opening my England career with three matches against the Rest of the World.

Our first match of the Currie Cup season was against the fiercest of rivals in Transvaal, and it was to be staged on the famous Wanderers ground in Johannesburg.

By then I should have been old enough and experienced enough to look after myself, but I made a foolish mistake. We had arrived in Jo'burg for afternoon practice the day before the game was due to begin. That night, the eve of my début for a new province, was as strong a candidate for a long sleep as any.

But I was so wrapped in the glamour of playing among Test

stars, boyhood heroes, such as Graeme and Peter Pollock, that I dropped my guard, went out on the town and arrived back at our hotel very late. The signs of giddiness were already beginning to manifest themselves, but I was confident that sleep would put me right.

I was wrong. The morning found me dizzier than ever, and I collapsed soon after getting up. A doctor was summoned and advised me not to play. His advice was sound, naturally enough, and common sense told me I would be mad to go on. But, in a mood of stubbornness, brought on partly by anger at my own stupidity the previous night and partly by desperation to make a good impression on my début, I insisted that I was fit to play.

We lost the toss and I found myself in the field immediately. The folly of playing was now obvious – I was violently dizzy again. But I kept my mouth shut about it all and forced myself on.

Peter Pollock was, at this stage, still at the peak of his fast-bowling career and, within his opening few overs, he had induced two edges. I caught them both at slip without the slightest trouble, but these catches were to be my only contribution to the contest.

A few minutes later my début for Eastern Province was over. I threw back my head, turned two helpless circles and slumped to the ground.

The drama of the moment was concealed by official reports that I had suffered an attack of sunstroke, but I cannot believe that that was glibly taken in by every one of the 8000 people in the ground.

Ali Bacher, the doctor who then captained both Transvaal and the South Africa side, raced on to the field and gave me an injection. I subsequently learned that he had been forewarned about my condition by Peter Pollock, and I can only be thankful that he was.

Even the injection was not enough to quieten me instantly, however. I'm told it took six or seven of my team-mates to hold me down until the fit had run its course.

Eastern Province, in fact, were close to a double tragedy. Peter Pollock had the presence of mind to put his hand in my mouth to release my tongue. Amid the frenzy, I apparently very nearly bit off his bowling finger.

When the needle had taken effect I was carried off, unconscious, and taken by Ali Bacher to the city hospital, where he got a top neurologist to examine me. For the next three days I was put through another series of tests. The match carried on without me and I was left with the depressing conviction that I had blown my big chance.

Purely through being too weak to look after myself on the eve of the match, I believed I had jeopardized my entire cricket career.

Everyone in the Eastern Province camp was consequently aware of my illness. They had all seen me throw a violent fit without even completing a single session with the province. They had every right, I reasoned, to discard me. Why should they take the risk? Why, come to that, should any other side now take a chance on me, knowing that this sort of trauma could be a regular occurrence.

My debt to Eastern Province is one I shall never forget. Despite it all, they welcomed me back into the team for the next match and never dropped me. I repaid them with a far more responsible approach. Since that fateful evening I have looked after myself and my condition with complete care, nursing myself through every bad patch and guaranteeing my presence on the field. But I am well aware that Eastern Province could, very easily and understandably, have slammed the door on me and altered the course of my life.

That was my one and only attack on a cricket ground, but it was serious enough to leave a lasting impression with at least one of my team-mates that day. Even now, every time I see the Pollocks they are swift to ask me if I'm taking my pills. They were shaken by the sight of my attack and the memory has obviously never completely left them.

My other major attack of recent years can be explained far more easily. With boredom the chief danger, I am never more prone to attacks than on long plane trips.

In March 1975 I arrived back in England after a brief family holiday in Australia following the MCC tour. The day after my return a small story appeared in the national newspapers reporting that I had been taken to hospital after collapsing at Heathrow Airport. I had been suffering from fatigue, it went on. In fact, I had had an epileptic fit.

It would never have happened if I hadn't made the mistake of locking my pills in my suitcase which, of course, was stowed away in the baggage compartment. I also had no sleeping pills, so, when the dizziness began in the latter part of the journey, I was helpless.

The routine was the same as always: a steadily worsening flickering in the corner of each eye, muddled thinking, but an active, racing mind. There was nothing I could do. Sleeping was out of the question without medicinal aids, so I just had to wait and pray that I could make it home.

My wife Donna and daughter Samantha were both with me, and, with Donna heavily pregnant with our second child, the last thing I wanted was to burden her with a dramatic collapse on board a plane.

We made it to Heathrow. Feeling desperately unwell, I somehow handled the inevitable interviews as we walked through the airport corridors, negotiated customs, then left Donna and Samantha waiting inside the arrivals building while I went off in search of the friends who had brought up my car.

I met them as arranged and all continued to go well as we opened the boot and began loading our luggage. By then it was too late to do anything but hope – even a pill could not stop it. I had told Donna how I felt and that there was no way I could drive home. All I needed was sleep.

Thinking back, it must have been a dreadful experience for both Donna, who understood, and Samantha, who didn't. They were watching helplessly through the glass front of the terminal lounge as my resistance collapsed and my body went with it.

Thankfully, the press had dispersed and an ambulance was brought alongside with a minimum of fuss. Donna and Samantha accompanied me to hospital and an injection put me right. Another lesson had been learned and I never travel by air nowadays without checking that I've got adequate supplies of epanutin and sleeping pills on my person.

In dealing with epilepsy, I have had to consider more than just myself. Donna was obviously in the picture long before we married and, at a very early stage, we discussed whether we should risk having children.

Different doctors have different theories on whether epilepsy can be hereditary, but basically they are all guessing. Once we had made the decision to start a family, there was obviously a worry involved. There still is.

But my thinking on this problem is perfectly straightforward. I have had a tremendous life, an enormous amount of enjoyment and considerable personal achievement, despite being an epileptic. If any of my kids were unfortunate enough to have the same trouble, I would be far better equipped to help them through it than my parents were and I see no reason why they should not be able to lead just as active and enjoyable a life as I have done.

By chance, I ran into a situation where my experience was invaluable. It involved my first bank manager, the man who talked me into buying my first house and supervised the opening of my first bank account in England.

He became a close friend and knew all there was to know about my condition. We had discussed its effects and problems a number of times, but one day he came to me in an obvious state of worry and confided that his son was passing out in exactly the same manner that I had done as a boy.

He asked me if I would speak to his son, and I readily agreed. I'm sure the boy was shaken when I told him that I had gone through exactly what he was suffering. He was keen on watching cricket and, as a current England player, I was no doubt something of a hero in his eyes. Finding that I had achieved so many of my aims while suffering from epilepsy was, I hope, a great comfort to him.

At the time he was depressed – understandably so. His life was as active as mine had been at the same age. He enjoyed swimming more than anything else and now he faced the prospect of being banned from the water. Along with his mates, he spent most weekends riding his bike and participating in the local scout camps. All that could be stripped from his life and I knew exactly what he was going through.

His parents were experiencing the same emotions of fear and panic that mine had done almost twenty years earlier and I believe I was able to help and reassure them too, simply by relating the full history of my condition and how I tackled it. The last I heard, parents and son were handling the problem very capably.

My attitude to epilepsy has moderated over the years. Where

once I was scared of the consequences and shy of telling anyone about it, I can now face it with a relaxed and open mind.

I don't mind who knows, now, because I am proud of the fact that I have achieved so much despite such a handicap. In a strange way I have been given added incentive. I have had something to prove, partly to others but chiefly to myself, and I feel I have proved it.

It sounds odd, I know. But being an epileptic just might have done my life a lot of good. It has taught me, for example, to be grateful that I am *only* an epileptic. I am, after all, suffering from an illness which can be controlled and arrested by medication. In that I am far more fortunate than countless others.

God has granted me the serenity to accept the things I cannot change and to live with my condition. Epilepsy does not mean the end of the world. If, because of my own experience, I have been able to get that message across to other sufferers, then I am grateful and, as long as I stay grateful, I can stay contented and I can cope.

2

Childhood

Greig grew up in the adventurous playground of South Africa's farms and coastlands, an endless paradise for a boy with his love of the outdoor life. Epilepsy affected, but failed to hinder, his childhood, and he freely accepts his fortune by comparison with the relatively claustrophobic upbringing of so many English children.

His boyhood story begins in his first Queenstown home, with his parents out for the evening and Guy Fawkes Night approaching fast.

I was only 7 years old when I almost burned down the family house and received an unforgettable thrashing for my efforts.

Young boys invariably become fascinated with matches at some stage of their childhood, and I was no exception. Maybe relatively few have played with fire with such disastrous results, however.

Guy Fawkes was a very big thing at the time, and I remember sitting at home listening to crackers and fireworks blasting off all around the neighbourhood and deciding that I was missing all the action.

Our servant was in the kitchen, acting as babysitter, when I came up with the idea of lighting a fire under my bed. Don't ask me why. It just seemed an exciting scheme to a frustrated 7-year-old.

I did have enough sense to pour water over my handiwork before the flames spread too far, and I went to bed that night feeling rather pleased with myself.

The servant, however, had found out about my operations and reported them to my parents when they arrived back at the house. I was immediately awakened by a disgruntled Dad. My mattress was taken away and put in the bath.

Dad duly doused the mattress and left it in the empty bath

before going off to bed himself, happy that any danger was past. Some time later, my mother woke up, complaining of being unable to breathe. Dad thought she was imagining it and told her so. Twice more she woke him and, on the third occasion, unable to bear it any longer, she switched on the light, finding to her horror that she could scarcely see her hand in front of her face. The bedroom was filled with smoke.

It needed only a glance down the corridor to ascertain that the bathroom was ablaze. The soaking in the bath had failed to extinguish the fire still burning inside the mattress and, as the household slept, the flames had escaped and spread.

Mother, young sister and myself were hurriedly collected and rushed outside to wait in the family car. As we sat there, underneath the big oak tree in the garden, Dad raced around frantically and the fire brigade arrived to control the blaze. But the house was already partially destroyed.

It was a long and frightening night for me, but the most lasting memory I have of the episode is what happened when morning arrived.

My father summoned me, having told mother to go out for a walk. She went, leaving behind her prize possession, a big, beautiful hairbrush that my grandfather had sent over to her from Scotland. Dad proceeded to break this brush on me.

The hiding was fully deserved and completely effective. For years afterwards I never touched another match.

Moving house was the next operation, and so it was that we arrived in a different part of Queenstown and a bigger house, which was to be the base for the family throughout my youth – days I shall never forget, whatever else may happen to me in life.

The house and surroundings lent themselves to the sort of existence I was to revel in. It was a big, rangy, single-storey building with spacious rooms and a huge lawn, flanked by trees. A stormwater drain protected one side of the property and the mountains climbed away in the foreground.

There was room to breathe, room to move. The house was away from the centre of Queenstown, which, in any case, was not a particularly big place. South Africa only has about half-a-dozen towns with a high population – Cape Town, Durban, Port Elizabeth, Jo'burg, East London and Bloemfontein – and the next category down contains hundreds of places just like Queenstown, with a white population of between 5000 and 10000.

Life there fell into a set pattern, although there was nothing boring about the routine. Schooldays I have already described, with the academic side over by lunchtime and the rest of the day devoted to activity on the sports field. Sunday was the only exception. This was a strictly-observed day of rest and there was literally nothing to do. Attendance at church was compulsory. I had to go at least once every Sunday and very often I went to both the morning and evening services.

Then there were the school holidays, the vacations that provided me with so many memories. In South Africa the school year was divided into four terms, rather than the three in England, and this consequently meant that we had four school holidays each year.

Christmas comes at the height of the South African summer and the custom, certainly for up-country families like ours, was to transport the entire household to the seaside, usually for four weeks of the six-week annual break.

The black servants were never neglected and one of the great sights at the beginning of our first holiday was to see the expressions on their faces as they saw the sea for the first time in their lives. They loved these breaks just us much as the rest of us, and they were made to feel a part of our family by being involved in everything we did.

For the duration of the holiday, home was a cottage on the cliffs overlooking the beach. Nothing glamorous, these cottages, just an old but habitable wooden building in which you carried oil lamps for lights, electricity being out of the question.

It was on one of these Christmas holidays that my mother nearly lost her life to the jaws of a shark.

We were staying at a place called Kei Mouth, on rugged coastland where the river Kei flows into the sea. A number of my mother's relatives were staying at the same place and, on this particular day, we noticed a certain murkiness in the sea water as we went in for our daily swim.

There had been storms up country throughout the previous week, which seemed to explain all, and we thought no more about it as we waded into the water – my mother, two aunts and myself.

We were by no means alone in the water. Several other families were further out than us, but we had been swimming no more than a few minutes when the shark attacked. It had ignored all the swimmers in front of us and, for some reason that will never be known, concentrated its attentions on my mother.

People regularly ask me how big this shark was and seem to relax when I tell them it was relatively small. But it has to be remembered that even this 'relatively small' creature was about seven feet long and capable of wholesale murder.

All I saw was a sudden flash of fin through the water, before a dreadful scream announced that the shark had struck. Its jaws were wrapped around my mother's right leg.

If the shark had opted for the savage, snapping approach at that moment, my mother would have stood no chance at all. But, instead of biting at her leg and taking chunks out of her, the shark apparently held her just below the knee and tried to pull her under.

One of my aunts grabbed her by the left hand and just hung on, while my mother struck out wildly with her right. One of two things then happened. She either caught the shark a painful blow in the eye, or distracted it so that it relaxed its grip on her leg and leaped at her hand. It made contact – but only just, and, with that departing bite, it was off into the distance.

It is very easy to talk casually of bravery against sharks. But I maintain that no one can predict what his or her reactions would be in such a crisis until it has actually been experienced.

To me, just 10 years old, it was perhaps the most appalling thing I had ever seen, and I think my immediate reaction was one born of the natural instinct of self-preservation. It all happened so rapidly that there was no time to think things out rationally. I ran.

On reaching the beach, I headed for the pub on the other side of the coast road, where I knew my Dad would be. Someone had got word to him of what had happened and, as I ran, panic still coursing through me, I saw him sprinting towards me.

In typical little-boy-lost style, I prepared to throw my arms wide and tell him what had happened. But his one aim was to reach my mother, and he rushed past, apparently without even noticing me. I turned to follow and got back to the spot on the beach where they had laid her out in time to witness an unforgettable scene.

My mother had huge white towels wrapped around her right leg, but blood was rushing out uncontrollably. It wasn't that sight which was to stay with me for years to come, though. As she lay, semi-conscious, on the sand, her arms were across her chest and her right hand – the one that had finally dismissed the shark – was an ugly distortion of what it had been five minutes earlier.

All her fingers were split down front and back and swollen beyond belief. It didn't look like a human hand at all.

Eventually a Land-Rover hurtled on to the beach and Mother was carried into it and taken away to hospital leaving me, alone and bewildered, to make my way up to my uncle's cottage.

Mother was in and out of hospital for the next two months, and only just escaped having to have her leg amputated. Even now, over twenty years later, she occasionally feels twinges of pain from it and gets some reaction from her mauled right hand.

Since that day, she has rarely swum in the sea. She used to love it, and spent most of her seaside holiday in the water. But, after that awful experience, the most she will ever do is paddle along the edge and certainly never goes into deep water.

I didn't go back in the water that day. Indeed, I stayed away for a number of days, until the mysterious murkiness had disappeared. But the accident did not deter me and, to the horror of my mother and family, I was soon swimming again without a moment of concern.

Even to this day, my mother goes berserk when she sees me go into the sea and simply disappear. I swim out for miles and, to date, I've never got into any difficulties.

Now and again, I suppose I wonder what might be underneath me. But my philosophy is that, if I'm unlucky, I'm going to be nabbed. It's not supposed to be a heroic attitude and I don't see it as foolish, either. I love swimming, I'm grateful to be able to swim capably and, ever since my epilepsy became apparent and I was told I should never again swim in the sea, I have been determined to carry on regardless.

After the attack on my mother, that particular stretch of coastline suffered a series of shark scares, which led to local discussion that it could be the same shark on each occasion. The guns came out, and I remember a lot of the local men going out on shark-shooting expeditions, intent on claiming retribution for these beach attacks.

It wasn't long before my family recovered from the shock, however, and, although my mother was still in considerable pain, I recall feeling mischievous enough to enter a fancy dress competition as 'shark bait', with my right leg and hand bandaged in exactly the way my mother's were. What's more, I won first prize!

Cricket played its part in these Christmas breaks by the sea — but an unorthodox form of cricket.

One of our relatives who was regularly at Kei Mouth with us was an uncle called 'Dummy' Taylor. In my later schooldays he was to influence my sporting life as a rugby coach. But, although rugby was his number one sport and the source of his nickname, his life was monopolized by physical activity.

He was one of the greatest competitors I have ever known, always wanting to take you on at one thing or another. At Kei Mouth, it was balcony cricket. Our pitch was suitated on the balcony of his cottage, which was very close to ours and consisted of a wicket and various pillars which you had to hit the ball past to score runs.

We played with a tennis ball, and a stump for a bat, and the games would go on for hours. I would often be up at dawn, running down the road to wait outside Dummy's cottage for the day's play to begin.

Whenever I have gone back to South Africa in recent years, and visited Dummy at Kei Mouth, we have always got the stump and ball out and played that game in just the same way we did when I was a holidaying schoolboy.

If Dummy Taylor was the Pied Piper figure for kids like myself during our seaside holidays, Rodney King made life one long, exhausting adventure during the rest of my school holidays each year.

Rodney was my cousin, single at the time and about fifteen years older than I. He ran a farm in the Tarkastad district where I used to spend, on average, three holidays a year. Rodney was the nearest thing I ever had to an idol and I used to follow him like a dog.

He had the ability to make life exciting for youngsters, by involving them in everything he did, setting them problems and simply keeping them active.

A typical day on the King farm would involve me getting up and being told that Rodney was worried about a flock of fifty sheep in a camp way out on the back of the farm – a distance of many miles. I would be asked to take a horse and ride out to the camp to count the sheep.

When I got there I would go round the pen, count, recount, then count once more before panicking because I could only find forty-five. After a final check, I would remount the horse for the long ride back, worried sick about the five missing sheep.

I would arrive back at the farm to give Rodney the dreadful news, whereupon his face would crack into a grin and I'd be put out of my misery. There were, of course, only forty-five sheep to be found. I would collapse in bed, relieved and exhausted, only to be shaken up at five in the morning in time for the milking session.

Farm life accelerated my progress into a man's world. I quickly learned to ride horses, and loved it after the inevitable discomfort of the early weeks. I was taught how to shoot, first with a pellet gun and then with real bullets. At 12 years old, I was even allowed to drive a car for the first time.

The discipline Rodney instilled, in his own way, came through with the use of guns. I was not only taught how to shoot, but when to shoot. In other words, the dangers were drummed into me so I would never consider abusing the privileges.

Just once, I let him down – and suffered for it. One morning, I argued with a friend of mine who was staying with us on the farm and, in a fit of schoolboy temper, I fired a few rounds of pellets into the ground around his feet.

A farmhand saw the incident and reported back to Rodney. Paul and I were summoned instantly. On occasions like this, there was never any question of apportioning blame. In his eyes, we had both been stupid and we both had to be punished, not by thrashing with a stick but by one of his inventive initiative tests. We were 'captured', 'imprisoned' and then left to work out our own means of escape.

Not everybody has been punished in that manner and I've no

doubt there are many who would not relish the challenge as we did. But, however much we might have enjoyed the achievement of getting free, the point had been made to us, and I have never let off a gun in anger or mischief from that day to this.

When we were finally allowed to use bullets, we were included in the farm shoots. These were exercises organized with a military precision, beginning in early morning with a drive to the top of the hill to check the position of whatever we were shooting – it might have been guinea fowl, buck or birds.

Rodney could have made all the necessary wind and position calculations without more than a moment's thought, but, again, he insisted on involving us, asking our opinions and making us feel important.

Sometimes, when we did strike lucky, the native youngsters (kwedini), who always followed us, would swoop on the dead animal and carry it away into the forest for a supper to which we were all invited.

Horse-riding got me into the odd scrape. Some of the horses on the farm were friskier than others and, if you picked a particularly lively animal, you needed to be very good indeed to stay on board.

I came off many times without serious injury, but once I had a very fortunate escape. Riding at fair speed alongside a river, my horse suddenly pulled up, shooting me over his head. Momentum carried the horse on and, as he stumbled, he very nearly landed on top of me.

I wasn't entirely cut off from the ball games I loved while on these farm trips. There was a tennis court on Rodney's farm and, throughout the week, challenges would be thrown out for the regular Sunday tournament.

Now and again, I would be the subject of challenges of a different nature. One that I have never forgotten concerns the time when a friend and I were dared to spend a night in a cow-shed on the farm.

We were allowed one pellet gun and one blanket and confined to the shed until dawn. If we lasted the course, ten shillings – a small fortune to us – was the reward.

I can't remember how long we did last, but I clearly recall being spooked by rattlings, squeaks and scuffling feet which, it later transpired, had not been rats or burglars but Rodney and his mates trying to frighten us. I think they succeeded!

On another night, Rodney woke me and told me to dress quickly. He explained that an old man had died on the neighbouring farm and it was up to us to check the place for any signs of foul play and rule out the possibility that he had been murdered.

I went along with him, quaking all the way, although in retrospect I'm sure he knew there was no danger. He just wanted to give me another adventure.

There was one occasion when I lost my temper at one of Rodney's teasing tricks and actually threatened to take a knife and kill him. My outburst was ignored that night and the next day I even refused to talk to anyone. Eventually, Rodney got me into the bathroom alone and talked some sense back into my head, telling me that, amid all the fun, I was going to have to be big enough to take a few character tests as well.

Like most good things, I appreciate those holidays now even more than I did at the time. I have since spent most of my time in England and frequently ask myself the question – what English boy could have been as lucky as I?

In South Africa, the rain usually came in thunder showers. The sky was almost constantly blue. Sport could go on undisturbed for twelve months of the year. Everyone swam and enjoyed it.

Shoots were organized regularly. Horses were readily available and the land was there to ride on. Not everyone loves the outdoor life, but those who do could not better South Africa as a childhood territory.

I've talked mostly about the holidays here, but in truth I enjoyed the term-time almost as much. Not that I showed it. Every time I came back from the farm, I would rush into the toilet, lock myself in and cry for hours. It upset my mother, I know, but it never lasted long and I was swiftly back in the school routine and looking forward to the next holiday.

Rodney King did not completely disappear from my life when I went to England and, when I was named as captain for the second Test against Australia in 1975, one of the first telegrams came from him. It wasn't just a passing word of congratulations, either, for when I walked out at Lord's to toss up with Ian

Chappell, Rodney and his wife were there in the stands.

He had booked a flight to England as soon as he heard the news, and I can't help reflecting that his 'adventure training' helped model the personality that was to play a large part in my cricket life.

It was during a winter holiday when Rodney was absent, however, that I experienced what may have been one of the most significant mishaps in my life.

As Rodney was taking his own family holiday on the coast, I spent this break at another farm, staying with a friend called Richard Sugden and his family.

Parties were reasonably frequent and, after one in a near-by village, Richard and I were driven home in a Chevrolet truck by the farm foreman. The route took us along a mountain road, treacherous after an evening of rain. Half-way back, the truck slid off the road and rolled over and over, down the mountainside.

Our descent ended with a thump against a tree, which at least saved us from a more unpleasant fate in the river at the bottom. The truck then lurched forward and came to rest in a ditch, throwing us from one end of the vehicle to the other and sending the back of my head against the dashboard.

Richard and I picked ourselves up, amazingly only bruised, but the great remaining worry was that the engine might explode with the three of us trapped inside. The only way out was through the window, which I proceeded to kick out with the heel of my shoe.

After scrambling clear ourselves, Richard and I helped out the foreman, who was hurt rather more severely than either of us.

For several days afterwards, I experienced a feeling that was soon to become horribly familiar. I was dizzy, still stunned by the blow on the back of my head.

That accident happened when I was 14 years old, and my first epileptic attack occurred less than a year later. To this day I wonder whether that accident and my epilepsy were connected or just coincidence.

3
The family

The eldest of four children, Tony Greig was lucky to grow up in a family of sports enthusiasts – and in an environment which did anything but cramp his development. It was also his great fortune in years to come that his father, Sandy, had been born in Scotland, qualifying Tony for a British passport and, ultimately, a place in the England team. The parents, four children and three full-time black servants grew into a happy and close-knit family, eventually overcoming together the single threat to their contentment. . . .

Smoking has a strange hold on me these days. I have often announced to the world that I've given it up. Then I decide to have a sociable cigar after dinner and, before I know it, I'm smoking almost as many cigars as I had previously smoked cigarettes. Once I had resumed smoking I seemed to lack the ability to control my intake of tobacco.

My father had the same problem with alcohol. In fact, he now admits and accepts that he is an alcoholic and I hasten to add that this is his admission and not an accusation on my part. What is more, he insists that he is still an alcoholic and will remain one for as long as he lives and that he has lost forever the power of choice of how much he can drink.

Often in the past he would tell us he had given up drink for good, but, as with my smoking, he would experiment again and, in no time at all, he was back to square one and in the squirrel cage again. The simple truth is that for many years he drank far too much for his own or the family's good.

I am convinced that for a long time he desperately wanted to give up drink, just as I wanted to give up smoking, but, while he was going through private hell, Mom was putting up with a lot and, as the eldest son, I assumed more responsibilities than many youngsters of my age.

Mom did everything in her power to protect Dad and her children, but there can be no doubt that this particular problem, while it lasted, affected all our lives.

As I reflect on those days now I realize the experience was probably beneficial in the long term. It certainly gave me an insight into some of life's problems and taught me a degree of tolerance and understanding.

As a united, happier family we can and do now laugh over the undoubted trauma of those difficult days and Dad is the first to concede that it took him far longer than it should to come to terms with his problem.

Until then – and since then for that matter – there were few problems he couldn't handle. Having joined the Royal Air Force in 1939 at the age of seventeen-and-a-half, he was a squadron leader at the age of twenty-one and had been awarded a DSO and a DFC in the red-hot cauldron of Bomber Command. He was posted to Queenstown at the end of 1943 and was chief instructor at the air training school there when he met Mom. They opted to remain in South Africa after their marriage and Dad became a well known and respected figure in business and sporting circles in Queenstown and further afield.

With that record behind him it was hardly surprising that Dad decided he would lick his alcoholic problem on his own. But he couldn't and inevitably had to admit that he was powerless over alcohol – that his life had become unmanageable.

That was the turning point in his and our lives. Happily there were many of his friends who had gone through a similar experience who were ready and willing to help him and, just as readily, he accepted their help and encouragement. There were relapses it is true, but it is a number of years now since Dad had his 'most recent' drink. He adamantly refuses to talk of his 'last' drink as he knows the insidious disease of alcoholism can never be cured, only arrested.

Today he lives a contented, completely sober life – but only one day at a time. He does it with the help of his friends in Alcoholics Anonymous and a deep spiritual faith which that fellowship has found for him. He has come to terms with his problem, with him-

B

self and with the world and he has never ceased to express his gratitude to Mom, his children and all those who stood by him in his time of trouble.

Coffee and coke are his only tipples today and he spends much of his time helping other alcoholics – but only if they seek help and are sincere in their desire to overcome this alcoholic problem. He has no quarrel with those who drink. That is their prerogative, he says, adding that alcohol is simply not for him – he can't handle it.

Obviously I am delighted and proud that Dad has arrested his problem, but it is a problem that has left a legacy. Today I have an apprehension of alcohol which amounts to fear – a healthy fear Dad says. I am certainly not averse to the odd beer or glass of wine, but I don't enjoy drinking hard liquor. At parties I am often concerned at the sight of others getting drunk. And while I appreciate, as Dad insists, that it is their prerogative to do so I don't enjoy the experience. I never will. Dad's experience with alcohol has ensured that.

Perhaps after all, though, Dad now has the laugh on me. He has his contented sobriety today, while I am still an inveterate smoker. It's a strange world. . . .

My first good fortune in life was to be born to two parents with long sporting backgrounds.

Dad had spent his schooldays at George Watson's College in Edinburgh, where the rugby rivalry with Heriot's and the Edinburgh Academy is very similar to the Queen's–Dale–St Andrew's–Selborne battle in my district of South Africa.

Apart from rugby, he played a lot of golf and soccer, and swam and boxed. Being Scotland, little cricket was played, but he did reach a reasonable standard in the game.

As I grew up in Queenstown, the College rugby team and the Swifts town side were both coached by my uncle, 'Dummy' Taylor, while my father ran the town's Under-19 squad. They became very successful, and I used to travel everywhere with them and even attend training sessions when Dad was in charge.

My mother Joyce was talented at any number of ball games. She played hockey, tennis and squash very well and, prior to my father's transfer, was ladies' captain elect at the Queenstown Golf Club, where, from a very early age, I used to caddy for her. Early in her golf career she had a hole in one, a feat which has eluded Dad for fifty years!

She would also play cricket with me in the garden and must have spent many hours bowling at me. But I have to admit that even when I was very small I was able to handle her without too many problems!

Despite their similar sporting histories, however, Mum and Dad differed enormously in their apparent attitudes towards my cricket.

If I was looking for praise, or soft encouragement, there was no point in going to Dad. He was always hyper-critical of every innings I played, every move I made – and he still is today.

He would rarely miss a school match in Queenstown. I would see him arrive every week and park himself in a shady spot to digest the proceedings silently. At the end of the day he always drove me home and, whether I had scored nought or 100, he would always pick faults. There would be no extravagant congratulations for a century, more often just a gruff criticism of a bad shot I played when I was on 55.

Although he has since sent me congratulatory telegrams when I've done well in a Test match, I cannot recall a single occasion when he has praised me to my face without adding some constructive criticism.

As a schoolboy I used to think it very unfair and there were times when I used to sit in the car and argue with him. Now, however, I can appreciate what a great help he was.

If I needed a few words of encouragement I knew I could get them from my mother – but she, too, saw the dangers of becoming too involved. I have since seen so many youngsters run into trouble through having parents who are blinkered so that they can only see their son and his talent, not realizing how much damage they can do to him. It has made me very grateful for the attitudes of my folks all those years ago.

Dad carried this stern line into formal family discipline. He was strict about my schoolwork and disturbed that I was never the brightest boy in the class. This could have been brought on by the fact that he had been a good scholar, and he could not understand why I wasn't so good.

I was by no means a dunce at school, but one of the subjects

I did have difficulty with was Afrikaans, simply through living in such an English home. Dad would accept no excuses and he packed me off to spend one of my precious holidays on an Afrikaans farm, where I had to speak their language all the time. I can't say I enjoyed the holiday, but I've no doubt it improved my Afrikaans.

He was also very fussy about personal tidiness. If ever he saw me hurl a newly-ironed shirt into the bottom of my clothes cupboard, he would go mad. Having lived in England for so long, I can appreciate his emotions, but at the time I found them hard to understand.

Children in South Africa have to do very little for themselves. White families such as ours have servants doing all the menial household chores, and it was unheard of, for instance, for me or my sisters to have to do the washing-up.

I only began to see how youngsters in other countries are disciplined into a household routine when I spent a year living in Scotland. My brother Ian and I were included on a roster for doing the washing-up, drying-up and stacking, and each day we had to bring in the coal. This was all foreign to us and the conclusion is an obvious one – South African kids are badly spoiled.

Donna may not agree, but I believe I have educated myself into a routine of personal tidiness over years spent in England. But if I had never left South Africa, I expect I would still be throwing shirts into cupboards without a thought for the work that had gone into getting them washed and pressed – for, at our Queenstown home, we even had a servant called Emily who would come in two or three times a week just to do all the ironing.

My sisters probably had similar problems, but, as I was three years older than Molly and seven years older than Sally, I learned the hard way and they were able to avoid my mistakes.

Both sisters were keen on sport, and it would certainly have been difficult for them not to be in our family. So much of our existence revolved around the sports field and, thinking back, I can't even recall any of my cousins not making a mark in at least one sport.

One of my great prides has always been teaching my brother to play cricket, and I enjoyed watching Ian improve under my direction.

Once, when I was 14 and he was a tiny 5-year-old, I recruited him to sort out an argument. Paul Ensor, one of my closest friends, was batting against me in our garden, with young Ian among the fielders.

Paul was a year younger than I and, as so often happens in schoolboy games, he protested that I was bowling too fast. I became annoyed by his constant complaints and made the rash assertion that my little brother could face me bowling at that speed. No chance, said Paul. So the challenge was taken up.

Ian, maybe a little bewildered, was brought up from his fielding position to put on a pair of pads. I walked back to the end of my longest run-up, determined to bowl flat out, but backing myself to serve up a half-volley. Sure enough, Ian stood in perfect position and played the ball back without any sign of concern.

He had jumped at the chance to play an active part in this 'senior' game, but I'm sure he was aware that if he backed out of the challenge and let me down I wouldn't easily have forgiven him.

Whether helped by my early coaching or not, Ian has since followed me to England and signed for Sussex. He has also done a three-year law course at Cambridge University, where he won a double blue and captained the cricket eleven.

His role in the garden cricket was generally that of a fielder, however. My sisters fielded, too, and often showed a good deal of annoyance at not being allowed to bat and bowl. Molly, in particular, would not accept my argument that girls didn't play cricket and I had plenty of fights with her on the subject, often ending up with her in tears.

They have both come a long way since those days. Sally married Phil Hodson, a Yorkshireman, who has played cricket for Cambridge and Yorkshire and they are living in Wakefield. They were married just before the drought which hit England not long ago and Wakefield became one of the first places in the country to have emergency standpipes erected. That at least gave me a line for an amusing telegram.

The only quarrel I have with Sally is that she has produced her first child in Yorkshire, and I'm not sure I approve of my nephew, Richard, playing cricket for Yorkshire !

Molly began a very successful marketing career within the chain of South African department stores known as the OK Bazaars and she has now moved on from there, after a spell in America, to advance that career.

There was one other chap who did take part in the garden cricket regularly. His real name is Teki Manzi, but to me he will always simply be Tackies.

Tackies is a black African who turned up on our doorstep one day looking for work. He was wearing nothing but a pair of khaki shorts and an old, scuffed pair of plimsolls, known in South Africa as tackies.

Dad decided to give him a job as gardener, but the appointment was not without its problems. We already had two black servants in residence, whom we considered part of the family. Sophie, a huge African woman, had worked in my grandmother's school hostel before coming to us. She did all the cooking, while her daughter, Nomketa, looked after the housework.

Sophie and Nomketa had their own quarters on the premises, but there simply wasn't any room for Tackies. So when he joined us, shortly after we had moved house, the first step was to give him some temporary space in the garage. We put up a partition at one end and then I helped him create his own bed out of cardboard. The only disadvantage was that we could no longer put the car in the garage!

Eventually, we built something more permanent around the back of the house and Tackies settled in as an addition to the family.

His duties included tending the garden, washing the car and many other outside jobs. But, in fact, he spent most of his time bowling to me in the garden.

Initially, he shied away from the games because he knew nothing about cricket. But, after watching my friends and me for some time, he thought he had worked out how to bowl and we let him join in. Tackies, however, was a blatant chucker.

Not only did he throw, but he threw fast, racing in with the typically wiry run of a black cricketer and hurling the ball down. He soon became quite capable, even if his bowling was illegal, and I was always keen to rope him in to give me some batting practice.

He would bowl to me for hours at a time, but was never keen

on batting. Sometimes he did have a go, when I wanted to bowl, but he was an amusing, completely uncoordinated sight at the crease.

While all this was going on, the garden was being neglected and we sometimes got complaints from my father. But I never underestimate the part Tackies played in these home-spun cricket games. He was an essential part of my story and he was recognized for it in 1977, when he left South Africa for the first time in his life and flew to London to appear in the *This Is Your Life* programme which featured me.

He stayed with Donna and me for a fortnight after the programme and spent every waking minute goggling wide-eyed at the sights of England. His favourite day was a sightseeing trip around London and I thought we were never going to drag him away from feeding the pigeons in Trafalgar Square.

So Tackies was generally my 'net' bowler. But, when the Test matches began, he would retreat to a fielding position in the outfield.

The garden Tests were played between my friends and me, with all the competitive fervour of the real thing. We would each select our country, then choose five batsmen and about the same number of bowlers. The games were organized properly and each team would bat until its five batsmen had been dismissed. The Tests were two-innings affairs that would go on from dawn to dusk, with the results counting towards a five-match rubber.

Naturally enough, most of my visiting mates wanted to be South Africa, but it may be significant that I was always happy to play as England.

My five batsmen would normally be Ken Barrington, Colin Cowdrey, Peter May, Ted Dexter and Trevor Bailey, and I would attempt to bat in the style of each player, from what I had read and heard about them.

When May and Cowdrey were in, I would try to drive and, if I lost wickets and needed a stout defensive innings, Bailey would be called up.

I even tried to copy the actions of the English bowlers when it was my turn to field and I remember Brian Statham opening my attack and Jim Laker coming on to bowl some off-breaks.

There was no opportunity for me actually to see these English players, except on their last tour to South Africa in 1964–65, when my father took me to East London to watch Border play MCC. As we stood in the queue outside the ground I peered through a hole in the wooden fence and my eyes fell immediately upon the figure of Colin Cowdrey, practising in the outfield.

From that moment on Cowdrey became a hero of mine and I followed his batting closest of all as I pored over the English scores in the newspapers.

Cowdrey was an ever-present in my garden team, and now and again I would pick some of the old-timers that my Dad had told me about, like Denis Compton and Len Hutton.

We generally used old cricket bats and tennis balls, but we stuck closely to the rules of cricket and improvised with one or two of our own.

The rubbish bin acted as our wicket; five yards behind it was a furrow which formed the start of the garden patch. Our rules stated that if you edged the ball into the garden patch without bouncing you were out, either caught by the wicket-keeper or at slip. You were also out caught if you hit any building or tree on the full.

These laws helped us to follow the coaching of our fathers and teachers and keep the ball on the ground. The other deterrent to smashing the ball in the air was the likelihood of breaking windows. Inevitably it happened now and again and the guilty batsman always had the cost deducted from his pocket-money.

Occasionally we would tire of cricket, throw down the bat and ball and turn to creating our own athletics meeting. Our house in Berry Street was encircled by a convenient stretch of grass on which we could concoct all sorts of events.

We regularly set up a hurdles course and, while somebody ran two laps of the house, he would be timed. You never ran flat out first time, because the idea was to keep breaking your record throughout the 'meeting'.

Then we would take down the hurdles and substitute a flat course of four laps around the house, timing each run again.

Golf was another favourite pastime. The Queenstown club was just a short walk from our home, and they encouraged youngsters to play as long as it wasn't at their busiest times.

The highspot came on Saturday mornings, when the club

staged a regular Youth Competition. I was never an outstanding golfer, so it was a great day for me when I finally succeeded in winning one of these tournaments.

Back in the garden, I never found myself stymied by being alone, because I had devised various methods of solo practising.

I could practise batting either by throwing a ball against the wall and hitting it on the rebound, or by tying a ball inside a sock and hanging it from the branch of a tree.

I knew the names of enough rugby players to stage individual rugby matches, too, and I would commentate as I pretended that I was being tackled, or that I was evading lunges and going through to score a try.

We had built some rugby posts out of bamboo and by constant practice I eventually became an efficient place kicker.

One of the greatest thrills, though, was listening to the Test match commentaries on our crackling transistor radios. When South Africa were playing in Australia the commentary would begin at the crack of dawn and, by five o'clock every day, I was sitting in my father's bed with a cup of coffee, listening to the match and to my father's dissertations on Don Bradman, who rivalled Vera Lynn as his greatest idol.

If it was England that South Africa were visiting, the time difference allowed us to listen during the day, but, as I sat in awe while the performances of Cowdrey were relayed, I never once imagined that I would one day be playing alongside him for England.

4
Schooldays

For one who freely confesses a revolutionary approach to many things in life, Greig is traditional almost to the point of being reactionary when it comes to education. Starting school when he had passed his sixth birthday, he progressed through the South African standards system, graduating from junior to senior school at 12 years old. He had two spells as a boarder, sampled the fagging system and approved. He doesn't pretend to have been an angel at school; indeed, boisterous behaviour more than once brought him a stinging backside. But he didn't resent the cane. Far from it. He feels that the phasing out of corporal punishment, both in schools and in the home, is a bad thing for discipline.

Maths was one of my father's pet subjects. It was, as he kept telling me, absolutely vital to my future life. Now, of course, I can see he was right, and appreciate the explosion when he discovered that my maths marks were not all they should have been.

At the time, though, I felt that he was being a shade harsh. After all, no boy enjoys having his father request his maths master to use whatever methods he deemed necessary until he felt he was making proper efforts to progress at the subject.

But that is exactly what occurred and, for some considerable time, he used the cane on me.

This teacher had always done his best by orthodox methods, but had failed to get through to me. Half the time I just wasn't concentrating, and during the other half I had probably been too lazy to do the groundwork.

When he turned to physical methods, however, I grew to hate him – yet my maths improved through a fear of the punishments. He literally taught me maths with a stick.

When I returned to Queen's to coach cricket many years later, we met up again and became good friends. We were able to laugh about the caning episode, but the significance of it was not lost on me.

I feel the importance of discipline in school and home very keenly. In my view, there are times when the best way to show a youngster that he has done something wrong – and deter him from repeating the misbehaviour – is by giving him a wallop.

Now, I'm not blithely advocating that every parent and every teacher should rush out and pick up sticks ready to punish their kids for the slightest spot of mischief.

Children are going to be troublesome, some more often than others, and there are many occasions when punishment by strong words or positive direction is far more valuable than a hiding.

As a parent, however, I will not hesitate to give one of my children a smack as a last resort. They don't enjoy it. They're not supposed to. The mere presence of the threat of a smack is often enough to make them think twice about the logic of being naughty.

I see no difference between corporal punishment at home and at school. If boys don't do their work properly, or if they flagrantly break school rules, they should know what will happen if they are caught and I believe the vast majority think of the cane as the ultimate deterrent.

There are rebels in every school and, at Queen's College, I dread to think what might have happened if the masters had not been permitted to use a stick as the final threat to the troublemakers.

I'm not preaching from any great height here. I have already quoted one instance when I felt the cane on my backside, and it was by no means an isolated incident in my school-life. I could be as rowdy as the next boy and I was caned more than once for fighting in the playgrounds.

School, for me, was as much an outlet for my sporting appetite as a place of learning. The academic side of life never came very easily to me and, although I was certainly not bottom of the class, there were a number of subjects in which I struggled badly.

We had exams at the end of every school term, but the end-of-year exams decided your fate. If you failed one of the two official languages, you were kept back for a year. I would not like to count the number of times I failed Afrikaans three times during the year then scraped through in the fourth exam.

Looking back on those years, I cannot fail to be impressed by the complete involvement of all the masters in every aspect of the life of the school and the pupils. The extra-mural activities like sport and music were all efficiently and enthusiastically supervised despite the fact that they were officially practised outside school hours.

Masters generally adopted a particular sport as a matter of course. It was expected of them and any who refused to co-operate would have been looking for another job before long.

Cricket at Queen's was divided into age-group teams and each year had its master-in-charge. He would usually supervise that particular age-group over a period of years, which led to a rivalry building up between the masters as well as the pupils.

If his side had won, a master would never be slow to make sure all his colleagues knew about it. If they had lost, he could expect a week of leg-pulling.

There was an even sterner competition between our masters and those of our opposition schools, and this, naturally, was transferred to the boys, adding to the incentives.

Just like their boys, the staff would finish lessons, eat their lunch, and within a very short while be out on the sports field. I am sure the majority enjoyed the involvement as they organized net practices with regimental efficiency and built everyone up towards the challenge of the following Saturday's match.

The point is, however, they accepted the fact that their job basically began when the sun came up and finished when the sun went down and the boys went home.

If the same level of application over and above academic responsibilities was still shown by the majority of English school-teachers, I believe that England's sporting stock as a nation would be far higher.

Maybe South Africa is more a participant country than England when it comes to sport. But why? I suggest much of it reflects on the schools.

Even given a certain enthusiasm for sport, boys need to be

directed, to have their talents channelled and a general interest shown in their progress. Otherwise, as happens all too frequently, sport just dies a sudden death as soon as the age is reached when social life expands.

Cricket provides a unique problem. Whereas an uninterested master could easily handle a football practice simply by supervising the picking of two teams, blowing a whistle and letting them play for an hour, cricket needs constant control, both in the form of coaching on technical points and simply directing the flow of batsmen and bowlers. In England, it seems, it is a lucky school indeed which has a supply of masters prepared to devote the necessary number of hours to cricket each week.

Their enthusiasm, in some cases, is understandably affected by the shortage of suitable facilities for the game. I know a number of English schools who now don't even run a cricket team, which may be because they can find no one to supervise it or maybe because they have nowhere to play. English county cricket needs every talented youngster who wants to take up the game as a career, and it saddens me to see possibly hundreds of potential county players lose interest in the game through the barriers put up by a lack of direction and a lack of facilities at school.

In South Africa, facilities are no more a problem than coaches. At my school, we had three squares for the weekend matches, eight turf nets and two concrete nets.

During our early years, we did most of our practising on concrete, which is, surprisingly, an ideal surface. As long as the concrete is smooth, it produces a fast, regular bounce and the ball can be hit because it comes on to the bat.

Twice a week we would practise on the grass nets and there would generally be one middle practice on Wednesday afternoons. The master-in-charge would always be present and on many occasions the headmaster would involve himself, walking around the nets and dropping a few words of advice and encouragement.

This went on throughout each summer as I climbed up the school ladder to the eventual peak of becoming first eleven captain. Yet I had been at school almost three years before I even took part in a competitive game of cricket.

I was into my seventh year when I joined the Queenstown Prep

School, and my first class teacher was a woman. No ordinary woman, though, for Audrey Walden-Smith was to be the first influence on my cricket career.

She was the teacher for all boys at the sub-A level – junior school first year – and she was very interested in cricket. But, at the time, no cricket was played by the youngest boys and our sport was confined mainly to rounders.

When I had moved on to Standard One, my third year at the school, a Sussex player, Jack Oakes, had come out as the senior school's cricket coach. Audrey got to know him and they formulated the idea of boys further down the school playing team cricket.

Together, they organized a team and arranged a match against the senior boys on the first-team ground. I played in that game, and have still experienced few greater thrills than walking out with the honour of knowing I was among the pioneers of the Queen's College youngsters. I can't remember the result of the match or anything else about it, but the occasion has always been a fond memory.

Soon afterwards, my age-group graduated from the Prep School to the newly-built Queen's College Junior School, and regular week-end cricket was quickly under way.

The first century of my life was not far away. It came in a 'derby' game against Cathcart, a very small school from a town just down the road, and was scored on what was known as 'the bunny field', a tiny ground with rough, coarse grass.

After I made that 130, my Dad told me that Vyv Sobey, the boss of Queenstown's main departmental store, wanted to see me in his office. Years earlier, he had promised me a bat if and when I scored a hundred and, sure enough, he had not forgotten.

I was shown into the shop and allowed to make my own choice. I ignored all the bats with autographs of famous players on them and chose one called The Barrier. It was to last me for years, through games on the lawn, holidays by the sea and, of course, school matches. All the family used it and I believe it's still around somewhere now.

My impatience was now increasing. I desperately wanted to go on playing cricket – I'd have played through the night if it was possible – and I remember regularly watching my uncle play for

Queenstown in the club league and wondering if I might ever reach that standard.

I got involved in any way I could, bowling to the club's batsmen just before they went out to the crease, operating the scoreboard and playing my own games against the pavilion wall while the big match went on in the middle.

It wasn't long, though, before many of my weekends were completely occupied with school sport.

Away matches in cricket, rugby and tennis were, in many cases, a weekend campaign, completely unlike anything that occurs in English schools. Our range of local opposition was small, whereas in England there are generally so many schools in any given area that the sports teams rarely have to travel more than fifty miles.

We frequently travelled upwards of 200 miles, which would mean either a car or train journey on the Friday night.

One of our biggest days of the year was the cricket fixture with Selborne College in East London, 140 miles away, and it provides a good example of the routine we became used to.

Both schools would field six cricket teams with, say, the under 13s, under 14s and under 15s playing at Selborne and the first, second and third elevens playing at Queen's.

We would board a train at Queenstown at nine o'clock on the Friday night, settle down in our sleeper bunks and pull out of the station about an hour later, reaching East London at about six o'clock on the Saturday morning. There we were met by the parents of our opposition, who would each take home one of our boys, give him breakfast, then make sure he got to the cricket ground on time.

Our matches were always all-day affairs and, when they were over, we would go back with the same set of parents, eat supper with them, then return to the station for another all-night trip, arriving back in Queenstown in time for church on Sunday morning.

These train trips would come round about four times a year for cricket alone and the first few were big adventures by themselves. Nobody would sleep a wink and at midnight we would get together for a feast in one compartment. There would be a continuous, excited chatter through the night and I now pity the poor masters who had to stay up all night making sure nobody got up to too much mischief.

I was as much an all-rounder then as I am now. I batted in the top order, bowled – generally seamers – and fielded either at slip or in the outfield.

But it was on one of the rare occasions when I bowled spinners that I found myself gaining selection for the South African School-boys squad for the first time. The wicket was wet and I decided to wrap my fingers around the ball and try a spell of fast off-breaks. The ploy brought me seven or eight wickets and my first major representative honour.

I shared the team captaincy with another boy during the early years, then gained promotion to the team one year ahead of him. Through this process I arrived in the first eleven at an unusually early age and played for them for a couple of years before being appointed skipper.

Somebody obviously thought I was cut out to be a leader even that early in life, for I also skippered the school's rugby and tennis teams at different times.

Rugby particularly appealed to me because, at first-team level, we were often watched by crowds of over 2000. Then, as now, a big crowd always lifted me. I find it far easier to concentrate and feel far more excited when there are 80000 people in the crowd, than when there are two dozen spectators dotted around the ground on a rainy day at The Oval.

I have often been called a 'big match player' and it is a term I cannot argue against. There somehow seems so much more point to the game when there is a big crowd. The motivation to succeed springs from their presence.

My first significant success as a leader came in rugby, when our first-team captain left the school and I was appointed skipper of a struggling side.

One of the departing captain's final matches had been a 15–0 beating by Selborne in East London, which was a shattering humiliation against one of our arch-rivals.

The fault, I believed, was not with our ability but our spirit, and it was this that I worked on as we approached the return match with Selborne on our own ground.

Our grandstand was packed that day and we turned on a great

performance to win 11–3. It was a remarkable turn of fortune in a short space of time and our coach summed up the reasons when he congratulated me. 'Our spirit was magnificent,' he said. 'It made all the difference.'

That was probably my first experience of such a man-management situation and it was to remain in my mind years later, first when I took on the captaincy of Sussex and then, two years later, when I was made captain of England.

However much ability a team possesses it can never fulfil its potential if the individuals are unhappy. Once you restore a happy spirit within the camp and turn the players into a family, then you are half-way to success.

By the time I finished school life, I was captain of cricket, rugby and tennis. I was also a prefect, which entitled me to the privilege of having three fags.

The fag system is often criticized, though more by those who haven't been through it than those who have. Personally, it did me no harm at all and, since I have left, my brother Ian has passed through the same system. At first he was apprehensive, but he left saying he would not have had it any other way.

At our school there was a permanent protection against the bullies who can and do abuse the fag system.

You began as a boarder in the junior hostel where, for your first year, you were a 'skunk', as fags were known, and given to one of the senior boys. You polished his shoes, cleaned out his cupboards, attended to his laundry – in fact, did virtually anything he told you to.

Then in the second year you were a completely free agent. You didn't fag for anybody and you didn't have one of your own. Boys in this stage were known for some reason as 'scum'.

In the third year you became a senior and an 'old skunk', with a 'skunk' of your own to order about. The catch came, though, when you had enjoyed that year of authority. For you then moved up into the senior hostel, and started the skunk–scum–old skunk syndrome all over again.

If you had made a habit of mistreating your fag in any way, the word would get around, and the third-years at the senior hostel would make life hell for you.

At first, I was a boarder for only two years, while my parents lived in East London. They returned to Queenstown just as I had completed my year as a scum, so I missed out on the year of luxury as an old skunk.

It all came good later, however, because I spent my last two years as a boarder and qualified for the trio of fags. All three saw me as something of an idol and I'm ashamed to admit that they did absolutely everything for me.

I used to be awakened in time to slide out of bed five minutes before the breakfast bell. I would step straight into the shoes and socks, carefully held for me. Number two fag would be standing with my shirt and tie and number three fag would have my trousers.

When I reached the wash-basin the toothpaste was already on my toothbrush and the towel ready and waiting. I could literally be out of the room and on my way to breakfast thirty-five seconds after swinging my legs out of bed.

They were all sports mad and would not have wanted to be the skunk of anyone else. They used to take a pride in my kit and would not let my rugby shirt go to the wash, insisting on scrubbing it and ironing it themselves until it almost shone. They polished my boots, cleaned my laces, then sat nudging their mothers every Saturday when I came out to play, pointing out how smart I looked.

At the skunk stage, I had been unlucky. My old skunk was a chap whose chief disadvantages were that he had little or no interest in sport and that he disliked beetroot.

One of the duties of a skunk, that could either be pleasant or not, was that you had to eat everything that your old skunk didn't like, due to the school rule that no food must be left on the plate. In return, he would help himself to something from your plate.

In our case, this didn't work out at all well for me. I seemed to spend my life eating beetroot, while he gorged himself on all the roast potatoes and meat from my meals.

It must have been an exceptional season for beetroot, because we seemed to get it with almost everything. Since that year, I have never touched beetroot.

Naturally, the system didn't work without its problems. There were bullies about, and some of them went unpunished. But generally I could find few faults with the life.

I was once seconded by a senior to help him practise his cricket. He knew I was reasonably good at the game, so he gave me a bat and put me up against a wall while he bowled fast.

He was a big fellow and considered to be the terrible tear-away bowler of the third team. But he was an old skunk, I was a skunk, and there was no way I could protest that he was bowling too fast.

So I stood there and took it as ball after ball flashed past my eyes, thumped against the wall and almost decapitated me on the rebound. I have to say, though, that it did me a lot of good. It taught me very early, purely through efforts at self-preservation, how to defend body and wicket against the hostile, short-pitched ball.

The 'skunking' system has recently been considerably modified at Queen's as a result of problems arising from abuse inherent in any such system.

5

Working a passage

Coincidences littered Greig's path from schoolboy to Sussex cricketer. But for a spot of alleged misbehaviour by his contemporary, Mike Procter, he might never have played for South African Schools. But for a severe attack of flu he would have been able to complete his final-year exams at Queen's College. If he had passed the two missing exams he would not have been forced to stay on an extra year and, thus, play for the national schools' side. And but for the unforgettable presence of epilepsy, Grieg would have been completing compulsory Army training instead of making plans for the momentous trek to England....

Lovers of the romantic adventure would probably like to hear that I grew up obsessed by an ambition to play cricket for a living. Well, I didn't – it never entered my head. Instead, I was convinced that my future lay in my native Queenstown as a history teacher.

History was easily my favourite academic subject at school and, because I enjoyed it, I became quite proficient. My headmaster wasted no time in trying to persuade me to come back to Queen's and teach.

My father approved of the scheme, seeing in it the long-term security that he wanted for me and, before I sat my final exams, a place had been secured for me at Rhodes University in Grahamstown – conditional, naturally, on my achieving the necessary grades.

It was at this point that a chain of events was set in motion that was to confuse these carefully laid plans and shape my future existence. All were unexpected, some were plain unpleasant. But, looking back, they were collectively fortuitous, forming the basis for my career in cricket.

The re-routing of my life began with a bad dose of flu. It could scarcely have come at a worse time, as I neared the end of the taxing finals. Just two papers remained to be written – commerce and my beloved history – but here I was, lying helplessly in bed.

At the time, the school's solution to my problem seemed a reasonable one. They didn't press me to get off my sick bed and complete the exams. Instead, they said, I could come back at the beginning of the following school year and write substitute papers on the two remaining subjects.

While I kicked my heels through the summer holiday period the results were announced. I had passed everything, including the Afrikaans paper, which had been the bane of my schooldays. But from a mood of high confidence I was plunged into panic when the school realized their earlier error and broke the news that I needed to sit every subject again to obtain a university pass.

The harsh nature of this decision only really came home to me when I failed Afrikaans at the second sitting and consequently had to return for another year at school and cram a completely different two-year finals course into a single year.

I doubt whether I have ever worked so hard as I did that year. Putting the apparent injustice of it all behind me, I flogged myself to extremes, using that university place – still a very vivid part of my dreams – as my own goal.

Despite the immense volume of necessary academic work, I found time to achieve further ambitions on the sports field. I had already captained the school at cricket and tennis, and now I was able to add rugby to the list.

For the fourth successive year I represented Border Schools in Nuffield Cricket Week, an annual tournament involving all the provincial school sides in the country and the highlight of the South African schools season.

Each province has its panel of selectors, comprising masters from the schools and a handful of coaches. They would generally hold a two-day trial involving a short-list of the outstanding boys, but the team for the Nuffield Week would ultimately be selected on the basis of performances through the season.

Caps, blazers and ties were presented to each of the fourteen

or fifteen boys chosen and the team would then travel by train to
the centre for the year's 'Week'. Accommodation for the week
was provided in hostels, and I well remember the growing sense
of excitement I felt each time I was picked.

The tournament received wide press coverage and was played
under the eyes of the South African Schools selectors. At the end
of the week a national team would be selected to play against the
senior side of the host province. If you were picked for this game
you received the South African Schools blazer, second in prestige
only to the full Springbok blazer.

During my first two Nuffield years I was playing with an age
group well above my own and it wasn't until my third attempt,
which was to have been my final school year, that I made a
serious challenge for the national squad.

Even then, I wouldn't have made it but for Mike Procter. I
can't now recall what his alleged misdemeanour was, but I clearly
remember him being out of favour during Nuffield Week and being
punished by omission from the South African Schools side.

Mike, even at that early stage, possessed considerable all-round
talents and was clearly destined for stardom. I wasn't in the same
bracket. In my own school back in Queenstown there was a
better batsman and a better bowler. But then, as now, I was able
to provide a telling contribution with bat or ball when the occasion demanded. The selectors obviously thought so, and I was
drafted into Procter's place for the match against the host province, Griqualand West.

The following year, detained at school somewhat against my
will, I was a more natural choice.

Nuffield Week that season was staged in Cape Town, and the
inclusion of the touring MCC Schools side made it a rather
special occasion. When it was over, Hylton Ackerman, later of
Northants, was named as captain of the national side, and
Norman Featherstone, who went on to play for Middlesex, was
also included.

The Western Province team which provided our opposition was
skippered by the then captain of South Africa, Peter van der
Merwe, and that match, on the famous Cape Town ground,
Newlands, remains one of the strongest reasons for not regretting
that enforced extra school year.

By the end of the season I was playing regularly for Border in the B Section of the Currie Cup. Prior to this, however, my thoughts had essentially been transferred back to the classroom for yet another sitting of final exams.

This time there were no mishaps and I reached the 'varsity pass standard. But, with my place at Rhodes awaiting me, fate applied another twist.

National Service was, and still is, compulsory in South Africa, and was then in the shape of a year's Army training. It had been planned that I would serve my year and then go on to university, but things didn't work out that way at all.

The Army turned me down and, although no specific reason was given, the assumption that I was exempted as an epileptic is an obvious one. Whatever the truth, it left me stranded with an empty year. Then, and only then, the thought of playing cricket in England entered my head.

As a passing thought it may have stood no chance but for the convenient presence of Sussex all-rounder, Mike Buss, as our cricket coach at Queen's. It is difficult, at this range, to set down my aims when I approached Mike and asked him if there might be an opportunity for me with Sussex during the next English season. Realistically, however, I can only have envisaged it as a time-filler before my return to academics at university.

Mike wrote to Sussex, putting my case. For weeks afterwards nothing happened, and he must have tired of my incessant pestering. Eventually the reply arrived. Tony Greig, they wrote, has not got a sensational school record, but if he is willing to pay his own fare, we will give him a year's trial at £15 per week.

The meaning was clear. Mike Buss was gambling on me, and that is something I have never forgotten. He may have been the first English coach to 'bring home' a South African schoolboy cricketer, and the responsibility he felt was later to be accentuated when we arrived at Hove.

For the moment, though, all was excitement. My father agreed that a season in English cricket would be useful and enlightening and pointed out that I would be able to visit my relatives in Scotland. But he made it very clear that I was to be back in good time to begin my university course, study for a BA and get some qualifications behind me.

My parents at that stage were in no position to pay my ticket to England, but I was lucky to be lent £125 by a very good friend of the family. That was enough for the single fare in a four-berth cabin on the *Pendennis Castle*. But I was told I must work to earn the money for some extra clothes.

My life up to then had been so concentrated within school and family that my wardrobe contained little more than school uniform, a sports jacket and my sports kit.

Christmas was past, three months remained before my scheduled departure for England, and I was desperately looking for a job. The students' holiday jobs had long since been snapped up and the best I could find was a post as junior messenger for the South African Railways at their diesel depot in East London.

If I say it was unglamorous, I'm being flattering. This was a job that seemed to have been almost created for the unemployed and, although I have no proof, it was firmly reputed to carry the lowest clerical wage in South Africa.

It brought me in the equivalent of slightly less than £20 a month. But that at least provided enough for me to get together a respectable collection of clothes for the voyage.

The chap I was succeeding spent the fortnight before his departure showing me the ropes with an excitement and enthusiasm that I humoured rather than appreciated.

He took me through the route around East London where I was to deliver letters and parcels. But he spent more care still when it came to demonstrating the process of counting letters before each delivery.

Left in charge at last, I dispatched my duties adequately but without any feeling for the job. Each day I would cycle to the depot, sort the letters, then cycle around the town. I rarely hurried due to the unworthy, but understandable, emotion that I wasn't being paid enough to worry.

Life went on in this tedious pattern for several weeks, until one day the local East London newspaper ran an article on me as a promising Border cricketer. It was picked up, read and passed around among the guys in my office and, from that moment on, I barely did a stroke of work.

Every day, when I came in, someone would have a cricket question to ask. By the time I'd answered it, someone else would come into the discussion and eventually the office would be at a virtual standstill. I can't even say I felt guilty about it.

My three months eventually expired and the moment I had been secretly dreading loomed uncomfortably close. It wasn't that I didn't want to go to England; on the contrary, my head had been full of the thought ever since Sussex had made the offer. My apprehension was simply centred around leaving my family for the first time in my life.

It was a tug at the heart that affects almost everybody when they make the first break from home. For me it was perhaps more acute than for many others, because our family was so very close.

I left with a confused and uncertain feeling, for, although I was due back within six months, I could be sure of nothing. It could be much sooner if I failed totally. It could be longer if things went so well that . . . but at that stage, this was the remotest thought.

I also left under disastrous circumstances which must have worried my parents sick. Only hours after I had waved the final farewells and boarded the *Pendennis Castle* with Michael Buss, a man went overboard and died.

The first Mike and I knew of the incident was the wailing of sirens as we sat eating our first dinner of the voyage, not far out of East London. When everyone had followed the emergency regulations and reported back to their cabins, a roll-call was taken. The missing man was Mike's cabin mate – which fact fell into place without too much puzzlement.

As soon as we had left the harbour, this chap had complained of feeling seasick, and he had looked appallingly unwell to boot.

I subsequently discovered that my parents were listening to the radio that evening when a newsflash announced that a man was missing, feared dead, from the *Pendennis Castle*. Heaven knows what must have flashed through their minds as they digested the news, but for a time they must have feared that my cricket career had been cut off before it had begun.

The rest of the voyage was less eventful, but an unforgettable adventure nevertheless. Ship life immediately appealed to me and, on a huge liner like the *Pendennis*, there was never a shortage of things to do.

It seems bizarre to think back now and recall that I still

addressed Mike Buss as 'sir' every time I spoke to him. Our age difference was no more than two years and, as I had left school, there was logically no longer any difference in our status. But the schoolboy tradition persisted. Mike was 'sir' or Mr Buss; and it was still unheard of for me to drink or smoke – the two most highly punishable offences back at Queen's.

Three weeks out from East London we sighted Southampton, and as we closed in on the quay Mike pointed out the two waiting figures who had come to meet us – his brother, Sussex fast bowler Tony, and Colonel P. C. Williams, then the Sussex secretary.

I felt I almost knew Tony Buss, although I had never set eyes on him before. Since being accepted by Sussex, I had spent a lot of time poring over the English cricket books and conducting my private studies on the cricketers I would be joining.

My first impression of Tony was an agile, athletic fast bowler. I was very wrong. Like his brother, Tony was a marvellous professional cricketer and a very fine bowler. But neither Tony nor Mike would ever pretend to be fleet-footed.

I felt flattered to be met by the county secretary, who then loaded my baggage and me into his car for the drive along the south coast to Brighton. It was late March, cold, bleak and grey, and the leaves were only just daring to expose themselves on the trees, yet the overwhelming impression of greenness that has always struck me when I return from abroad was the first thing I noticed about England.

The journey from Southampton to Brighton took a considerable time in those days, long before the south coast motorways were built, and I suppose Colonel Williams and I must have shared a reasonable amount of conversation. My thoughts, though, were ahead of us at Hove. I could scarcely wait to see the county ground, meet the players and discover the place that was to be my new home, for six months at least.

In fact, I can remember only one comment that was passed during the drive – and I remember it as if it were yesterday. Colonel Williams looked up from the road and advised me that it was sure to be a marvellously hot summer. When I asked him how he could be so sure, he waved a hand at the skeleton trees and explained that the crows' nests were higher than usual. It was my introduction to the beliefs and folklore of the English countryside.

My first fortnight in Sussex was spent at the home of Alan Oakman, a senior professional in the side and the first in the long line of Sussex players who had coached at Queen's College for a spell. Alan remembered me from his time in South Africa and took me under his wing until all was prepared for me to move into digs.

I don't believe I could ever have found a better landlady if I had scoured the whole of England. Mrs Flo Cooper, a middle-aged Yorkshire woman, lives just 200 yards from the county ground gates, and treats every cricketer who comes into her house as a son.

I am just one of a stack of Sussex cricketers who have stayed with her, yet I saw her almost as a second mother. Her food was good and her hospitality incomparable – there would always be a bed and never a complaint if I came back from a trip without warning.

More than ten years have passed since I moved in with Mrs Cooper but she hasn't shaken off the Greigs yet. During the 1977 season, my young brother Ian joined the Sussex staff and followed my footsteps into Mrs Cooper's home.

People often ask me the first things I noticed as I began to explore England. The answer is simply that I didn't. In the early days, all I knew was the path between Mrs Cooper's house and the county ground. It was all I wanted to know.

April was an appalling month that year. Snow fell regularly, but it couldn't douse my enthusiasm and curiosity. I had heard so much about the movement a seam bowler could produce in English conditions that I was determined to experiment, whatever the conditions. So I took a ball out into the Hove nets and bowled on to a thick matting of snow.

I later heard that I had been watched with some bewilderment by Tony Buss and Ken Suttle, who had quietly agreed between themselves that I would 'soon learn'.

Lord's was an obvious target for a wide-eyed 19-year-old and I made the journey up to London with snow falling again. I had no idea that the ground was the subject of strict security measures, or that you needed MCC permission even to set foot on the sacred turf.

I marched up to the Grace Gates and walked boldly in. Wandering round by the Tavern, I caught my first glimpse of the famous old pavilion, rising austerely into the gloom of that April morning.

To play at Lord's was still a private dream. To captain England there against Australia was a laughable fantasy. So, in case I never had the opportunity again, I jumped over the fence, strolled on to the playing area and calmly picked up a handful of Lord's grass to send home to my parents.

There were no angry shouts from the MCC offices. No one materialized to frog-march me off the premises. It never entered my head that they might.

I left the ground as casually as I had entered and I still don't know if the gatemen simply didn't see me or if they assumed that I was a far more important visitor than an inquisitive county trialist come to steal some of their precious grass.

At long last the season got under way, and I found myself with a full schedule of second XI, club and ground and benefit fixtures. Not that it worried me. I would have played every day if it had been possible.

It was Kenny Suttle's benefit year and, as the John Player League was not even thought of, Sundays almost invariably found a Sussex XI performing somewhere around the county to raise money for Ken.

I played in most of these games and enjoyed them enormously. As a second XI trialist, I was expected to do most of the work while the senior professionals took it easy, but that was fine with me. I was glad just to be on the same field as the stars of Sussex and the England Test players, such as Fred Trueman, who often guested.

My record in the second team was far from impressive. I made one or two useful scores and bowled capably on occasions, but did nothing to suggest that I might have a big future in the game. All the time, I was conscious of the impending return to South Africa and university, and the need to save enough from my £15 a week to afford the boat fare back. Naturally, I wasn't able to live royally even if I had known how to.

Sussex had probably seen little in their own fixtures to persuade them I was worth persevering with, but two representative games changed their mind.

The first was for Colonel Stevens's XI against Cambridge University, which would generally have been regarded as a match of fairly minor importance. To me, however, it is significant for two reasons : first, that the Colonel's team was captained by Mike Brearley and, second, that I scored a century in each innings.

This was my first meeting with Mike Brearley, a man and cricketer with whom I was to develop a close affinity and deep respect a decade later. In 1966, however, all I knew was that he was looked upon as an England batsman.

I remember little of my first hundred in that match. But, in the second innings, I can clearly recall going out to bat, with Mike, who had opened, still at the other end.

Runs came quickly and the thought that I might score my second century seemed to occur to Mike before me. He did everything to help, giving me the strike whenever possible, coming down the wicket to offer advice and generally shepherding me into three figures.

Later in the season I was included in Arthur Gilligan's XI for the fixture against the touring West Indians – a match that put me under the English public eye for the first time.

My success came with the ball, when I took the wickets of Rohan Kanhai and Conrad Hunte in a satisfying spell of seamers. A number of Sussex committee men were present at the game and it seems they saw enough. At the end of the season I was called into the county office and offered a three-year contract starting the following summer.

The lure of university had been waning within me throughout this trial season at Hove. I had enjoyed myself so much that I found it difficult to reconcile myself to the thought of returning for another three years of studies. The offer of a contract seemed a godsend.

First, however, I had to convince my father, which was no easy task. I spoke to him by telephone from England and outlined the offer and all it meant. He seemed singularly unimpressed both by the pay and the prospects, but he obviously sensed that I yearned to be given a chance. Finally he relented and laid down an ultimatum which I never forgot. You have four years to make the grade as a top-class cricketer, he told me. If you fail, you get out and find a job with more security.

It was a realistic assessment of the situation I found myself in, and one we would both advise every father who lets his son go into cricket to consider adopting.

The last thing my Dad wanted was to allow me to drift around, playing a few games of cricket and stagnating as a mediocre county cricketer with a limited number of years ahead of me in the game. By setting a time limit he was giving me an escape route if things went wrong. Neither of us imagined that, before those four years were up, I would be playing for England against the Rest of the World.

To comply with the residential qualification rule, I was to be allowed home for only two months. Having chosen the Christmas period for my return, I then settled into a winter job in the family department store complex in Scotland.

Cricket had occupied me so completely during the summer that it was September before I had any opportunity to visit the Scottish countryside about which my father had told me so much. My grandfather, who owned the stores, gave me a job in the main branch at Bathgate, near Edinburgh, but, being similar in character to my father, he insisted that I began at the bottom of the ladder.

I started work in the electrical department with responsibility for delivering, installing and collecting television sets which we rented out. Occasionally, I was let loose on the sales side in the store, which normally led to a protracted discussion on the family history of the Greigs from customers who would grow curious about my accent and ask who I was. By the time I left the store I don't think there was much I didn't know about my ancestry.

Every job has its headaches. Mine arrived every time a family failed to pay the rent on their television and I was dispatched like a reluctant bailiff to retrieve the set.

I witnessed some heart-breaking scenes among the city slums, where large families lived in sparsely furnished flats with only the television for comfort. I felt cheap and cruel as I denied them their simple single pleasure, and once, sympathy and conscience drove professional duty out of my mind.

There was nothing new about the scene as I drove up in the firm's van. Another block of tenement flats, dirty and impersonal, and an indigent family who couldn't pay for their viewing. But, somehow, this one was different.

When I walked into the flat, the depression surrounded me. There were six lads, all watching the television, while their mother tried to keep the place in some semblance of order. It wasn't that difficult to tidy up, because there was no furniture left – they had lost it all to the bailiffs.

Outside, the city shambled away despairingly. It was a rough area and there was nowhere for the kids to go, nothing for them to do. If I had taken the television I could have been responsible for a suicide – the place was that bad.

I left empty-handed and drove back to the store lost in a mix of grief for that family and guilt over my failure to complete what should have been a straightforward collection.

Back at Bathgate, I was given a lecture by the store manager. If everyone behaved like this, he told me, we wouldn't have a business at all.

I went back to the flat the following day and confronted the mother with an ultimatum that was more a plea than a threat. I explained that, if I valued my job, I should just pick up the set and go, but told her that she must do everything to get the money together. I even offered to loan it to her myself.

Eventually, they did scrape the rent together and they kept their television. But I wasn't sorry when the bailiff role passed out of my life.

Weekends in Scotland were unforgettable. My grandfather lent me his Daimler, and I felt a thrill of wealth and importance as I drove away into the lochs and highlands.

Christmas approached quickly and, as Sussex included one return fare to South Africa in the contract, I was able to fly home. The holiday was marvellous and, before I flew out again, I took a long pep talk from my Dad.

The goodbyes were perhaps more emotional here than they had been a year earlier. I was still basically a family boy, yet I was setting off on an adventure that was likely to keep me away from home for three years.

My brother was growing up fast and had enjoyed every

moment of my stay at home, as we played endless games of cricket in the garden. As I said goodbye to him at the airport I saw that his eyes were wide and misty. I reached out to shake him by the hand and felt two huge tears drop on to my knuckles. I had to turn and walk away.

6

Sussex

Back in England for the 1967 season, Greig, now 20, ran into an undercurrent of resentment at Hove. The lanky young blond fellow from South Africa's farming country was seen almost as an impostor by some of the traditionalist figures in the Sussex camp – and as a threat by some of the older players whose place he was now contesting. The need to prove himself was now paramount, as Greig felt a stranger for the first time in his life.

Jim Parks senior, coach to the Sussex side and father of our new captain, typified the establishment ideal in approach and appearance.

He was an extraordinary man who liked to remain aloof from his players, rather as an army major would segregate himself from his troops. Jim was Sussex to the core and carried the county next to his heart. As a player he had been a resounding success and as a coach he had much that was useful to impart.

But my abiding memory of this somewhat imposing character is of the day in 1966 when Malcolm Sylvester was given a trial.

Sylvester was a South African who had come to England a few months after me, invited by another of the Sussex new breed, Peter Ledden. At 26, Malcolm had reached an age when he needed to make an immediate and powerful impact if Sussex, or any other county, were to consider him a worthwhile investment. I had the feeling they gave him a trial as a favour, and I think he knew it.

He was, however, a man who instantly endeared himself to the rest of us. A big, hearty individual who had a smile for the world and a worry over nothing, Malcolm had that something which compelled you to like him.

On the day of his trial we agreed to give him a half-hour

c

warm-up in the nets before the coach arrived. It seemed a good idea as the big fellow grew in confidence and began to smash the ball all over the ground. He was batting brilliantly as the familiar figure of J. H. Parks strolled across the grass towards the nets.

The routine went much as normal for a while. Without more than a nod or a word of greeting, Jim Parks senior stationed himself just outside the net in his customary attire of MCC blazer and sweater, then bent to pick a ball from the blue Sussex box and shone it absently as he took in the proceedings.

Sylvester was still destroying everything we could bowl at him and obviously loving every minute of it, particularly now that the coach had made his entrance and his trial was officially under way.

Nothing went right, however, from the moment that J. H. Parks surprised us all by removing his faithful blazer.

Hanging it carefully on one of the net poles, Parks walked back to the bowlers' stump and marked himself a short run. The usual babble of net chatter altered its pitch now as we stood back dutifully for the coach and waited with an anticipation that, I have to confess, was tinged with amusement.

Parks was no longer as young or as fit as he would have liked and with his middle-aged physique and short-cropped grey hair, he looked anything but the demon bowler. Sylvester tapped his bat eagerly and the rest of us looked on like schoolboys hoping to see teacher made to look silly.

A gently curving inswinger followed his slow, wobbling approach and Sylvester, drunk with confidence, saw the green light. Thrusting his foot at the pitch of the ball, he aimed to club it fiercely in the extra-cover direction.

Whether his form had rushed blood to his head, or whether there was more in the Parks delivery than we could see, no one can tell – although I suspect the former. For Sylvester's bat scythed through on the wrong line, the ball sliced off a thick inside edge and lobbed back to the bowler.

Parks took the catch as if he had expected nothing else, dropped the ball back into the box, retrieved his blazer from the pole and stood back. It was the most effective piece of confidence destruction I had ever seen.

The trial could have been abandoned on the spot, for Sylvester just went to pieces. The punchy, free-flowing shots disappeared into a mess of uncertain prodding and swishing at air. Quite frankly, he played like an idiot.

The coach eventually took his leave, having seen his trialist fail under the sort of pressure I am convinced he could never have banked on producing.

Being an easy-going sort, Malcolm was able to laugh it all off. The trial had not been essential to his life-style; failure was not a disaster. He ended up back home in Johannesburg selling baked beans.

I never did manage to break down the surface of old Jim Parks and establish any relationship. It was the same story with a number of the Sussex characters of the time. In truth, I sometimes felt a little lonely, a figure apart among names I had read about and faces I recognized from books and faded newspaper cuttings back home in Queenstown.

Strange really, because an odd coincidence on the day after my initial arrival in England had made me feel very much at home.

After spending the night at Alan Oakman's house, I caught a bus to the county ground, intending to explore my new surroundings and meet as many of the players and officials as possible.

Walking in through the main gate, I branched left towards the secretary's office just as a man began to descend the office steps towards me. He was wearing a tie which I recognized immediately as that of the Queen's College Old Boys.

It seemed an extraordinary episode to me, travelling half-way across the world only to bump into somebody from my old school, and I gratefully made myself known to the man, Reuben Levenson, whom I later came to know well.

During that first season at Hove, I would often go into the Long Stop bar on the ground for an evening drink and feel a great sense of pride to be standing among the stars. Jim Parks, the Nawab of Pataudi, Ted Dexter and the great players from the visiting teams would always cluster in there after a day's play and swap stories. I lingered on the outside, not because they deliberately ignored me, but because I was the raw newcomer, unsure of himself, unproven, yet longing to be part of it all.

When the second team didn't have a fixture, the trialists and young professionals were expected to report to Hove. If the first XI were involved there in a county match we would be given duties, and mine was usually to work the scoreboard.

This was something I enjoyed doing, because it gave me a chance to watch the best English players in action, and also helped me to recognize them. I soon had to learn, because part of the job involved identifying the fielder by numbers after each ball – and the spectators were never pleased when they spotted a mistake.

In 1967 I opened my contractual period by scoring a century on my first XI début, in the opening Championship match of the season. And if that sounds a bland statement of fact it is grossly misleading.

Speculation about first-team places was rife from 1 April, the date on which everyone reported back from their winter jobs. Ken Suttle, Alan Oakman, Les Lenham and Graham Cooper were all drawing towards the end of their careers and there was considerable conjecture that they might be phased out in favour of the younger players such as Peter Graves, Peter Ledden, Mike Buss . . . and myself.

I suppose a certain amount of tension is inevitable whenever a team approaches a transitional stage and players' positions, even livelihoods, are at stake. In this case, the tension was so noticeable that even I, the rookie, could sense and feel it permeating through our pre-season training.

My only aim was to make sure that I was included in that side for the opening match. I hadn't a clue who was most threatened by my presence and I didn't really care.

What I did care about quite passionately was the fact that both Mike Buss and his brother, Tony, were becoming the subject of a good deal of unfair pressure, Mike because he had brought me to the county and Tony because he supported his brother's judgement.

Ultimately, I believe, this worked in my favour, giving me a greater incentive to justify my presence in the squad, thereby vindicating the man who had given me this chance in the eyes of his critics.

The first indication I was given of my selection came one morning after training, as I sat with captain Jim Parks in the Gondolier café near the ground.

This was the traditional morning stop-off for many of the Sussex players and, as we drank hot chocolate, Jim revealed that it was his intention to give me a run at number five in the batting order. He didn't state categorically that I would be in the team for the opening match, but, as he told me not to worry if I got one or two low scores early on, the inference was obvious.

Our first Championship fixture was against Lancashire at Hove, beginning on a Wednesday, and the previous night's Brighton *Evening Argus* confirmed my hopes with a story about my inclusion in the Sussex side.

Lancashire had finished 12th in the Championship the previous year, two places below us. But all I knew of them was that they possessed perhaps the best opening attack in the country – Brian Statham, whom I had so often made blind attempts to impersonate in our garden cricket Tests at home, and Ken Higgs, recently established as a regular in the England team.

Try as I might, I can remember little about one of the greatest days of my life. The weather is a blank, the crowd were just a blur – I haven't a clue how many people were present. All I remember is the incredible thrill of justifying myself.

Sussex won the toss and ran into immediate trouble. My turn to bat came sooner than I had expected, for we had lost three wickets in reaching 39.

Statham was bowling up the Hove slope and causing all sorts of problems. His first ball was too good for me. It beat my defensive stroke, pitched on my foot and set up a confident yell for l.b.w., which umpire Dusty Rhodes rejected.

Later that day I was to have a revealing chat in the bar with Dusty. He told me that he had spent a good deal of time in South Africa, knew Queenstown well and had met my father a number of times. He even knew the name of the barman in our local pub. I'm not suggesting his decision was influenced, but I'm glad that it was Dusty Rhodes and no other umpire who adjudicated on my first ball in county cricket. . . .

Statham hit me on the toe again with the second ball, but this time there had been a distinct inside edge to stifle any appeal. From then on, my head went down and I lost myself in a single-minded bid for success.

My first target was 50. In fact it was my only target, and when I got there I was so overjoyed I couldn't have cared if I'd been bowled next ball. It never occurred to me that I should start all over again, aim for a century and steer Sussex towards 300. I relaxed, opened my shoulders and started smashing the ball around. Suddenly, I was in the nineties and the notorious nerves hit me like a sledgehammer.

For a time I slipped back into uncertainty, as if I had suddenly become aware of what I was doing, the impudence of it all. The century was achieved by stutters rather than strides, but once into three figures I was off again.

I remember no particular shots. It even strains my memory to recall how I was out – slogging at the off-spinner I think. But the welcome I received back at the pavilion will always live with me.

Standing at the bottom of the pavilion steps were the Buss brothers, Michael in front and Tony close behind him. Relief and pleasure were etched in their expressions as they clapped me on the back and the knowledge that I had taken a weight from their shoulders gave me, in turn, still greater satisfaction.

I thought, too, of my parents, who were that day sailing to England, prior to living in Scotland for two years. News of my innings was broadcast on the BBC sports programmes which were relayed to the ship, but my name, apparently, was mispronounced, so my folks had to wait impatiently for confirmation.

I had finished with 156 and Sussex had totalled more than 300. A perfect opening day to the season was concluded by John Snow rifling four quick wickets in the final session to leave us in complete command.

The day wasn't over for me, though. Our dressing-room was besieged by press and radio reporters and they all wanted interviews with me. It was bewildering, but I admit I enjoyed it – probably too much. Rain fell steadily for the next two days and, with no further live cricket to report, all the papers carried follow-up stories on the boy from South Africa.

Every time I walked into the pub, my hand was shaken and my

back slapped by dozens of people I had never seen before. By the end of that three-day period I had been brainwashed into believing that I was really quite something.

Although I didn't think so at the time, what I needed more than anything else was my father. He would have dragged me away from the backslappers, led me out of the ground and reminded me of the idiot shots I had played during my innings. He might just have said, 'Well done' without reservations for the first time in his life, but there would have been no chance of me leaving him with the impression that I was a star.

In retrospect I appreciate that I was nothing special and that what happened next was the best possible way in which to close a dangerous chapter.

Our next match was at Cambridge, against the University, and because it was so early in the season and we had lost most of the Lancashire match to the weather, the entire first team was picked.

More than 2000 people turned up on the first day and I remember thinking with appalling arrogance that they must all have come to see me. Among the crowd was a chap called Chris Danziger, who had been one of my cricket masters back at Queen's. He was doing a post-graduate course at Cambridge and I was pleased to see him as it gave me another chance to relate the story of my century, while we stood talking before play began.

We batted first and all our early batsmen got into some sort of form. I went in at five again to face the off-spinner David Acfield, who is now with Essex. Acfield had played in the M C C Schools side which had toured South Africa a couple of years previously and, purely on that evidence, I wrote him off.

My attitude was that if I could score 156 against Lancashire's Test match bowlers, why should a university off-spinner worry me? It was an awful approach to an innings and I paid dearly for it.

Acfield pitched the first ball outside the off-stump and it turned enough to beat my brash cover-drive and bowl me.

Alan Oakman was at the dressing-room door when I shambled back, demanding a guinea for a Primary Club tie – presented to county players recording their first duck. A guinea was a sizeable chunk of my humble wage, but losing that hurt me far less than the humiliation of showing myself up in front of all those people.

I had to force myself to go back and meet Mr Danziger as arranged and, as I produced a sheepish grin, I'm sure I detected a glint in his eye that told me a great deal. I wasn't as good as I had allowed myself to believe.

With the realization that I couldn't walk on water came a more sensible level of application. For the rest of the season I devoted myself to the task of scoring 1000 runs.

In South Africa, the most common news we had received of English county cricket concerned those who had passed 1000 runs, or which bowlers were approaching 100 wickets. It was obviously the thing to do and I became obsessed with the ambition.

Every night I would go back to Mrs Cooper's, or to my hotel room if we were playing away, and sit down with pen and paper to calculate how many runs I still needed and what I would have to average if I batted in all our remaining innings.

I made it – but only just and I cannot pretend that the season continued in the fairy-tale fashion which had begun it. I scored one more century, against Gloucestershire at Bristol, and took eight for 25 in a spell of seamers against the same opposition at Hove.

Those bowling figures are still my best, and the 156 I scored in my first Championship innings was to remain the highest of my career until I had played more than forty Tests.

I had planned upon another winter working in the family store in Scotland and that, indeed, was how it began. But bad news brought a pleasant surprise. My grandfather became ill, and when my father was told he decided to bring the entire family up to Edinburgh. So instead of the three-year separation I had feared, I was reunited with all my folks only nine months after leaving them.

It wasn't for long, though. Shortly before Christmas, I was invited to go on a miniature world tour, being organized by Joe Lister, who is now secretary at Yorkshire. I accepted without a second thought.

Touring has long since become a part of my life, but, as with most things, I shall never forget the first one.

It was a three-month affair, starting in Sierra Leone. We were to play in Kenya, Uganda, Pakistan, India, Ceylon, Singapore,

Bangkok and Hong Kong – and the reality was as stunning as the promise.

The touring party was dominated by players who had just missed selection for MCC's winter trip to the West Indies. Captained by Mickey Stewart of Surrey, it could have been classed as an England B team, with a bowling attack headed by Harold Rhodes – fierce and at his peak – Geoff Arnold and Derek Underwood, and a batting line-up which included Mike Denness, Keith Fletcher, Dennis Amiss and Sussex's Ken Suttle.

This was my first link with men like Fletcher and Amiss, who were to become such close friends in the years ahead, and with Denness, with whom I was to be so involved during his painful experiences as England captain, and later when he managed WSC's World XI.

The cricket was of variable standard, which didn't concern me too much because I missed half of it anyway! I was hit on the hand while fielding in Bombay and, after playing through the following match in considerable pain, I had the injury properly examined. A broken bone was discovered and the hand was put in plaster. Joe Lister gave me the option of flying home or staying on with the party to complete the trip. That didn't need any consideration – I stayed.

Ironically, the match I completed with the bone broken was in Madras, where I scored a century before the biggest cricket crowd I had ever seen. I was to have a good deal more experience of Indian crowds in tours to come, but on that occasion the experience was breathtaking.

Our playing record on that trip was impressive and, when we arrived back in England, a challenge was issued to Colin Cowdrey's MCC team, recently returned from the Caribbean. For obvious reasons the challenge was declined, which was a pity. We believed we had a very fair chance.

Before accepting Joe Lister's invitation I had had to sort out a delicate passport problem. My South African passport would have had me barred from several of the countries we planned to visit, but the South African government were understandably reluctant to allow their citizens simply to change 'nationalities'. They suggested, in fact, that I was being 'disloyal' and threatened to withdraw my citizenship.

With no solution forthcoming, I had taken it upon myself to apply for and obtain a British passport, but on returning to England I decided to do things properly. I wrote to the South African Minister of the Interior, explaining my position, and eventually received a reply giving me official permission to use a British passport. So ever since then I have been in the unusual position of possessing both South African and British passports.

My immediate priority now was to ensure my full fitness for the start of another English season. I was forced to keep the plaster on my arm for much longer than expected, but it was removed in time for me to complete the customary April training programme and take my place in the side.

Sussex, however, were in for a season of unrest. The politics in which the county club was becoming embroiled were all still a mystery to me. But even I could not ignore the fact that the team were not ideally happy.

Jim Parks was eventually relieved of the captaincy and the committee's choice as successor was an unfortunate one.

I compare the appointment of Mike Griffith at Sussex with that of Mike Denness as England skipper. Neither man was ready for the responsibility.

Griffith was a respectable county batsman with the right Sussex background. He was a Cambridge graduate and his father 'Billy' was prominent in the hierarchy of both the county club and MCC. As a man I liked him a good deal. But being a good bloke with the correct upbringing has no bearing on the qualifications for a cricket captain.

The people who appointed him were doing what they thought was best – of that I have no doubt. But a good many of the players felt quite strongly that Tony Buss, four years older and considerably more experienced at county level, should have been appointed. The result was a lot of discontent.

In the circumstances, we didn't have an unprofitable season, thanks to a run in the Gillette Cup which carried us into the final against Warwickshire.

Sussex had won the Gillette in the first two seasons of its existence and, even now, the very mention of the word Gillette seems to rouse the members and followers.

The 1968 season was kept alive by that run, and I believe to this day that we should have won the final. We made only a moderate score, but Warwickshire were flailing hopelessly until A. C. Smith got them off the hook with an innings of chance shots that we should never have allowed to succeed.

In the Championship the high spots were few. I recall only one vividly, and it was provided by a man who could make the rest of us look the merest novices when he turned his mind to it – Ted Dexter.

Ted had retired from Test cricket in mid 1965 and resigned the Sussex captaincy months later. But, after dabbling briefly and unsuccessfully in politics, cricket lured him once again.

England were having a bad time and the public demand for Dexter's return grew steadily. Finally, he made himself available for Sussex again, and I remember the bustle of activity before our Championship match with Kent at Hastings.

I can't vouch for its authenticity, but the story goes that our twelfth man was sent out from the ground to clear a runway of sorts so that Ted could land his private plane.

When he strode into the dressing-room, a strange smell accompanied him. It was his cricket case, unchanged after three years of semi-retirement and suffering severely from mould and dry rot.

There was nothing comparably rotten about his batting. Dexter blatantly relished the new challenge and marched out on a Hastings turner to give Derek Underwood hell. I have never seen Underwood punished so severely, either before or since, as Ted lorded it to a double-century without a second thought for reputations. He even used the same old, brown bat that had accompanied him to the wicket when last he played regularly.

The mere presence of Dexter made Sussex feel a team again. I have met few people who look the part of a cricketer quite as Ted did, and his stature brought confidence seeping back into the side. We were to face a few more lean years, however, before the tide began to turn.

7

Donna

In a climax fit for a fairy-tale, Greig married the girl from down the road, Donna Reed, in March 1971 after a romance that was at times anything but idyllic. They eventually lived luxuriously in a rambling house in Sussex and the impression of affluence was accentuated by Greig's new Jaguar. He cheerfully explodes the myth, explaining that the house was a property gamble that put him heavily in debt and the car was a loan from a garage. Material assets now include two children, Samantha and Mark, who arrived to cement a marriage that survived its share of traumas before arriving at its current happy state. For the past two years they have lived in the splendid Sydney suburb of Vaucluse, overlooking the harbour, bridge and opera house.

They say there is a moment in everyone's life when they realize it is time to settle down. It happened to me on a March morning in 1970 when I landed in London after a tour of the West Indies and discovered that Donna Reed had left the country.

I remember feeling a sensation of shock and then being surprised at myself. It wasn't, after all, as if Donna and I had ever talked of marriage at that stage. I was 23, she was 20 and our romance had been conducted at an express pace with more goodbyes than anything, as we both followed our careers.

Short of actually living in the next house to us, Donna was a perfect candidate for the girl-next-door situation. Her family lived in Queenstown and became very friendly with mine and, although I never dated her during schooldays, she was often at our house to see my sister Molly, who was a class-mate.

We grew naturally apart as I concentrated my attentions on my impending trip to England and I thought no more about

Donna until her name was mentioned in a letter from my parents while I was touring with Joe Lister's side.

My family were in Scotland at the time, my father working in the store business, and Donna had phoned them during a holiday in Britain. She had apparently been to finishing school in Switzerland – which made me raise an impressed eyebrow – but had since returned to South Africa.

I made a mental note to catch up with her one day and carried on with my cricket. My chance arose after the 1968 English season, when I was accepted as coach to my old school in Queenstown. I found Donna working in the town and we were soon going out together regularly.

The following summer Donna secured a place at Lucy Clayton's modelling school in London, then moved to Brighton to work as a freelance model. The romance went on.

But, while Donna's work in England continued, I then faced a hectic winter schedule in the 1969–70 off-season. A term coaching at Queen's was followed by a Caribbean tour with the Duke of Norfolk's XI, captained by Colin Cowdrey. It was a useful and enjoyable winter, but it reduced our relationship to letter-writing.

On the flight back to London I turned to thoughts of England, the new season with Sussex . . . and Donna. I presumptuously expected to find her waiting for me and I was oddly stunned when a phone-call from Heathrow informed me that she had left to work in Switzerland.

That March morning was another crossroads in my life. If I had accepted the news with disappointed resignation and the thought that we were bound to meet again soon, I doubt whether Donna and I would now be happily married. She had gone, I later found out, because she had understandably tired of my constant flitting around the world. Her flight to Switzerland was as much a planned test of my character as a journey to a new job.

Without even leaving the airport buildings, I booked a seat on the next flight to Geneva and, before the day was out, I was sitting on the train which circles the huge and beautiful Lake Geneva.

I had managed to discover Donna's new address, and phoned her there when I arrived in Geneva. Saving explanations for later, she directed me to a station she called 'Bay' . . . at least that's what it sounded like.

The train wound around the lake and began the ascent into the Alps, finally coming to rest at a station called 'Bex', which left me in complete confusion. Eventually, I was told that Bex is pronounced Bay and stepped off on to the snow-covered platform.

Donna was waiting for me and my heart performed one or two physical jerks as I wondered how I was to be received. Deciding on the positive approach, I set off down the platform at a gallop, throwing my arms apart to bury her in a welcoming hug.

I hadn't reckoned on the ice beneath the surface. About five yards from my target, my feet parted company with the platform and I lurched on to my backside. Momentum carried me sliding onwards, knocking Donna's legs from underneath her and bringing her crashing down on top of me in a welcome far more intimate than ever I could have planned.

With the need for forced reunions overtaken by laughter from the fall, we were able to sort out our differences over a meal later that night.

Donna was working in a superb mountainside hotel and, as we walked back after eating, I was still marvelling at the snow, which I had never experienced in such volume before. It wasn't long before I had a closer look, stepping on what seemed like solid ground only to find it was a deepish hole covered over by snow. For the second time in a matter of hours I found myself lying helplessly in the snow with Donna laughing at me.

We returned to England together before the new season and Donna's parents followed, to spend the summer in Brighton. For me, it was a summer of the big breakthrough as I made it into the England side against the Rest of the World. But disappointment was soon to follow with exclusion from the MCC party to tour Australia under Ray Illingworth. I was looking for a job again, and it meant another return to South Africa.

Donna travelled back at the same time, but her father, exercising parental caution, persuaded her to accompany her parents on one boat while I followed on another.

We were to meet up again in Cape Town a fortnight later, and I waited for the reunion smugly. I had bought Donna an expensive watch as a present and confidently expected it to impress and delight her. But it wasn't to be. I left the watch in a case, lying on my bed, and when I went to pick it up just prior to landing it had gone.

I strongly suspected that the cabin boy had stolen it and, in a fit of rage, I re-boarded the boat and sought him out. All the threats I could muster failed to shake him, though, and Donna got a lame sob-story instead of a present.

Donna's winter work was in Cape Town. I was hundreds of miles away, coaching at St Andrew's College in Grahamstown. Soon, the position became intolerable and I persuaded Donna to come and join me for a few days – long enough, in fact, for me to propose to her.

Accepted by the girl, I then had the unpleasant part . . . asking the father for his daughter's hand. There was nothing especially formidable about Mr Reed, but I would rather face all the world's quickest bowlers in turn than go through that ordeal again.

I'm sure he knew why I had come to see him, and there was no foreseeable reason why he should refuse me, but I still suffered an awful attack of nerves as I put the question to him while Donna and her mother stood outside in the corridor with their ears to the door.

We were married in March of 1971, four months after getting engaged, and the wedding was a bigger affair than either of us had anticipated. The invitations list seemed to grow endlessly, multiplying our piles of presents to almost embarrassing proportions.

It sounds awful I know, but our honeymoon was not a great success. It wasn't long before impatience began to grow in us both – an impatience that called us back to England where we could start to build a home and each continue working.

We flew back in early April, stopping briefly in Athens on the way. Our first home was a rented flat in Brighton, but the summer was a frustrating one as I watched Richard Hutton take the all-rounder's place in the England team.

Cricket, however, was an undoubted help to our marriage in its initial, most difficult, stage. I had become used to travelling about, loving the free and exciting life and never really knowing where I was bound. I had no doubts that Donna was the right choice, but the process of stabilizing my existence and getting used to living with the girl came hard. It is probably the same for many couples, but, for a while at least, I needed to keep moving.

Donna was becoming increasingly involved in public relations work and leading her own life, so the brief but frequent separations caused by cricket allowed us to remain very much as individuals. It was good for us, and we were happy to go on that way indefinitely – until Donna became pregnant for the first time.

The months before Samantha's birth were the most depressing and most taxing of our marriage. Donna was reduced to a bleak misery. She took to wearing a black tracksuit as her pregnancy outfit, and rarely took it off. She became so introverted and dejected that I once told her to go back to her mother.

The hard times ended with the birth. A child, I suppose, can make or break a marriage that has suffered such a trauma. It made ours, without any question.

Samantha's arrival, and the subsequent birth of our son Mark, have made it progressively more difficult for me to leave the family. Not just more difficult, but more unpleasant.

When you become a professional cricketer, the travel is one of the hazards you accept. But because you have accepted it doesn't mean it is easy to tell your kids that their Dad is off for another week, fortnight or, come November, four or five months.

At first, it was easy. Donna and I took Samantha everywhere while she was in the carry-cot stage, and she travelled around the world twice before she was old enough to realize what it meant.

It is when they start walking, talking and thinking that the problems arise. The time comes for them to go to nursery school, then day school – and once that begins, it is neither easy nor desirable to unsettle them with winter trips abroad.

This is the common plight of the professional cricketer, who is only employed at home for six months of the year. To find winter work he invariably has to travel abroad, either to South Africa or Australia. It is often a wrench, but essential in order to maintain a standard of living and develop security for the future.

Towards the end of my career I found it increasingly hard to fly off into the sunshine and ignore the fact that I was missing the delights of watching my children grow up. These thoughts made a major contribution to the important decisions I took with regard to Kerry Packer's project in 1977.

Packer's series also made unconditional provision for wives and families – a far cry from the disgraceful attitudes of the English cricket authorities on this subject.

Players are discouraged from bringing their wives at all on an England trip but, if they ignore the mutterings, they can obtain permission to have their wives with them for twenty-one days – just three weeks out of a tour that may go on for twenty-one weeks.

I could understand this thinking if the authorities were shouldering the costs of bringing out the wives. But it doesn't cost them a penny. If players want their wives to be with them, they have to fork out a great deal of money – but that is their responsibility, not that of the Lord's committees.

I consider the twenty-one-day restriction an appalling encroachment on the privileges of every married man, and my feelings were never a secret to the men in power in the English cricket hierarchy.

There are people in the game – some players among them – who harbour fears that wives and children could take over a cricket tour and turn it into a holiday camp. I can understand that apprehension and there is no doubt that certain guidelines must be adhered to.

The fact that a player's wife is with him should never mean that he has an excuse for missing a net or a team meeting. Discipline must be maintained and, more important still, the spirit of togetherness that plays such a huge part in a team's success must not be affected by the wives' presence.

But the vast majority of professional cricketers are sensible, adult men. If they are on a tour, the cricket and the team would always come first and I think such fears are groundless.

In my experience, a number of England cricketers have been of far greater value to the team when their wives have arrived.

Geoff Arnold was miserable without his wife on the 1974–5 tour of Australia. His cricket suffered and he was ultimately left out of the side. I don't think he would have completed this tour if his wife had not flown out and, when she arrived, he was a different man.

Alan Knott is another good example of a player who performs

better and contributes more to team spirit when his wife, Jan, has joined him.

When Mike Denness captained the MCC side in Australia in 1974–75 the twenty-one-day rule was strictly applied. If we wanted to keep our wives in the country for a longer period we were instructed that they must stay in a separate hotel, away from the team.

Donna came out in the middle of the trip and, when our three-week allowance ran out, I booked her into a hotel a short walk away from where the team were staying.

Each evening after play I would report to the team room for the daily meeting, share a drink with the boys, then slip out to meet my wife, feeling like a criminal escaping from Wormwood Scrubs.

Usually, I would spend the night with her, then get up early to walk back to the team hotel in time for breakfast.

I am sure that was not what the authorities intended when they enforced the three-week regulation, and I'm equally sure it did nothing for my fitness or peace of mind.

But when you make rules like that one, you ask people to behave more like schoolboys than grown men.

Donna, for her part, always coped amazingly well with all the problems of being a cricketer's wife – problems which my father had, sensibly, but forcibly, pointed out to us before we married.

8

South Africa

Being born a South African has not always been a blessing in Greig's life. He has found himself cast by some as an impostor in England and a deserter in his homeland. He has been insulted by catcalls around the grounds of England and by the occasional rash of abusive anonymous letters – never in greater volume than in the summer of 1976, when he threatened to make the West Indian grovel and unwittingly provided the anti-Greig, anti-South Africa factions with free ammunition. Greig's views on the conflict in South Africa and on the morals of apartheid have never wavered. He still loves the country, but the prospect of confrontation appals him. . . .

South Africa is afflicted by a simmering racial uncertainty which convinces me of one thing – as long as the current situation prevails, I will never take my family back there to live.

Despite all that has happened to me in various parts of the world during the last decade, I have always been conscious of the fact that I am still a South African. Donna retains the same affinity, yet, however much our hearts yearn to return, our heads overrule them. The risks are simply too great at present.

There are a great many things going on in South Africa that I cannot condone and, if the wrongs are not rapidly corrected, the prospect of violent confrontation must be faced. It is a prospect of which I want no part.

I don't want to fight anyone and I am not prepared to commit my children to a situation in which they may quickly find themselves involved in a war.

The thought that I should become a martyr in the cause of my country is, to my mind, a stupid one. I consider myself fortunate to have open options. Wherever we settle, the door is always open for a trip to South Africa.

No one denies that South Africa is a troubled country, but those who view it from afar have no way of knowing that there are many people at government level trying to do the right thing, striving to find an effective and just solution which is acceptable to blacks and whites.

While they work unobtrusively, the extremists claim the headlines and influence the beliefs and the judgements of newspaper readers both inside the country and abroad.

It is always the policy of the world's press – and understandably so – to feature sensation and controversy. If someone makes an outrageous statement about South Africa, he will win himself a big headline. The danger, of course, is that the average reader goes off with the impression that extremists express the common beliefs of the South African leaders and people.

The only way to discover the truth about the country is through first-hand experience. But in the current climate I would not recommend anyone to settle there without having a long hard look first.

Naturally, I retain a fervent hope that the situation can be resolved peacefully. Even now, the country is moving towards black rule. If the natural evolution is allowed to continue this must be the end result for, just as in Rhodesia, the blacks hold a massive majority in terms of numbers.

The fear is that the blacks will become frustrated with the inevitably slow process and force a confrontation in which violence can no longer be avoided.

Power cannot simply be handed to the blacks overnight, however, for the obvious reason that they are, as a race, not yet capable of exercising that power democratically. Of course, they possess many educated men with qualities of leadership, but in general they still need to be further educated and to be seen to be capable of putting that education to good use.

If a way cannot swiftly be found in which to achieve this desirable state I fear the worst for my country in years to come.

South Africa was just as controversial while I was growing up there, but a number of circumstances combined to protect me from any real awareness of the problem.

Queenstown was a relatively small country community, far removed from the areas where violence was a likelihood. My father was a progressive man, with a reputation for treating his black servants well, and any of his children who were caught abusing or mistreating a black child would be punished instantly.

Dad taught me to count my blessings and appreciate a standard of living that, certainly for a white boy like myself, must have been incomparable in the world at that time.

I was basically ignorant of the arguments that raged over South Africa in the outside world because, to me, a black boy was no different from a white boy.

Tackies, our gardener, and Sophie and Nomketa, our cook and housekeeper, were part of the family and I was glad to have them as such. The fact that they were black seemed completely irrelevant.

During my school holidays on the farms, black boys became my friends and it would never have occurred to me to treat them as anything but equals. I spoke their language fluently and we spent endless happy days riding and hunting.

In the woods where they made their homes, we would stage prolonged games of cowboys and crooks, in which it was always the cowboys who were painted as the goodies chasing the crooks out of town. More often than not, I think I ended up as the crook!

I often joined them back at their huts and shared a delicious meal which I can best describe as porridge with sour milk. The racial issues that were even then causing strife and controversy in other parts of the country seemed so far away that none of us gave them a thought.

Perhaps they respected me more because of my father's well-known kindness towards the blacks, but there was certainly never a hint of resentment or nastiness of any kind.

I understood enough, however, to realize that their standard of living could not even be compared to mine, and I felt genuinely sorry for them. Throughout my life, I have retained a sympathy for the poorer black people and I would always help any of them in any way possible.

Occasionally, we would hear of outbreaks of violence in the

troubled districts, but at that stage it all meant little to me. The nearest I came to witnessing any sort of unpleasantness was in seeing blacks, obviously imprisoned, being herded around in what amounted to labour camps.

It was natural, then, that when I went to England to begin my cricket career, I would defend South Africa in conversation. I had plenty of opportunity, for, in the late sixties, the subject was especially relevant to cricket, with growing conjecture over the severance of sporting relations with South Africa.

I argued the South African case on the grounds that it was impossible to understand the problems unless your life revolved around the country – and to give credence to my views I quoted the case of my cousin.

Rodney King had devoted his life to his farm. He had built it into something worthwhile, a security for his family in years ahead. But, all the while, he had employed black farmhands, treated them well and given them a decent living. Was it right that he should be expected to throw away everything he had worked for? .

I never attempted to support South Africa on moral grounds because I could never have done it with any sincerity. I had grown to deplore the petty apartheid policies of the country, which were made more apparent to me as I began to see different attitudes around the world.

The enforcement of separate park benches for blacks, and separate entrances to the post offices and the cricket grounds, was simply absurd and degrading, and the subsequent phasing-out of these and similar regulations was welcomed by every peace-loving person in the country.

My verbal protection for South Africa was natural enough for a teenager suddenly finding himself in a country where many people were hostile to the system under which he had been born and raised.

So I felt oddly contrary in later years when I returned periodically to South Africa and found myself standing up for England. It wasn't that I had transferred my patriotic allegiances, simply that I recognized the same symptoms there as I had seen at first in England. Just as the English, and the rest of the world, allow themselves to be swayed by what they read about South Africa, so South Africans too often blindly accept that the newspapers tell them all there is to know about England.

I pointed out that the country was not brought to a standstill by daily strikes and that every British child did not grow into a vicious soccer hooligan . . . impressions that had obviously been all too easy to accept on the evidence of the press.

It was an unusual situation to find myself in, trying to dissuade people in two very different countries from assuming blinkered opinions about each other. It was an early insight for me into the power of the press, something that I was to feel at a far more personal level before too long.

Just as I accepted the moral deficiencies of South Africa, however, so it is only right to put on record the fact that I believe there is a lot lacking in England.

There is a general lack of discipline in both school and home – something that has far more serious consequences than some people might be willing to accept.

I can make a fairly accurate assessment of youngsters' manners around the world, because I come into contact with so many of them. Even through the minor duties of a cricketer, such as signing autographs, I have been in a position to observe kids' behaviour – and England is generally very low on the list.

Without the correct amount of discipline, a child can degenerate from noticeable yet harmless ills, like impoliteness, to far more serious instances of vandalism.

Teaching standards in England also concerned me. I believed I needed to be a near-millionaire to secure the kind of education I wanted for my children, as it is far less of a risk to choose a good private school than take a chance among the state schools, where one may be good and another down the road quite inadequate.

Maybe the shortage of good teachers reflects in another way the lack of incentive in England to work hard and master your profession. In South Africa or Australia, someone who is willing to put in a lot of hours and reach the top in his business will reap the rewards. In England, that doesn't seem to follow at all.

One could go on picking faults in any country, but I have a lot for which to be thankful to England, the country which gave me a chance in international cricket which I would have missed completely had I stayed on in South Africa.

The tragedy of my native country could never be ignored, however, and after about four years in England I was glad to be offered the chance to air my views on the controversy.

My opportunity arose through a televised debate, centred on the South African issue and featuring boxer Henry Cooper, golfer Max Faulkner and myself. It was around this time that the anti-apartheid demonstrations of Peter Hain and his followers were at their peak, and I knew that what I had to say would cause something of a stir.

I didn't have to wait long. The debate, naturally enough, soon swung to the subject of Hain and my opinion was sought through a question from the audience in Brighton Polytechnic's main hall.

Primarily through the disruptive influence of Hain's clan, a number of tours to and from South Africa had been cancelled, and a Springbok rugby tour of England had been seriously obstructed. I am quite sure the audience expected me to come out with an attack on Hain and all he stood for, but I didn't – I said I thought he had done a good job for the people of South Africa.

Most of the audience were probably cricket and rugby fans, whose spectating had been cut and inconvenienced by Hain's activities, and their reaction was a predictable mix of puzzlement and dismay. But, to forestall a further barrage of follow-up questions, I insisted on being allowed a quiet hearing to put my points. This was the first time I had ever been confronted with the issue by a national medium such as television and I considered it vital that I made my thinking quite plain.

My first point was that I did not necessarily agree with all Mr Hain's methods – in fact, I strongly disapproved of them on the occasions when he had resorted to violence. His campaign was supposedly in the interests of human rights and there was no way he could justify the random use of strongarm tactics in a cause aimed at peaceful integration.

The fact remained, I went on, that he had been responsible, in some cases directly and in others indirectly, for the introduction of sporting sanctions that were to have a greater impact on South Africa than any arms or food embargo could ever have had.

South Africa is, to all intents and purposes, self-sufficient, and the sort of sanctions that were imposed on Rhodesia – cutting off supplies of essential materials – would have had little or no effect. So Hain chose to involve international sport and, immediately, touched the most delicate part of a South African's emotions.

The South African people live for sport and with sport to a degree that I have not seen equalled in any other country in the world. They will tolerate a good many shortages and inconveniences in other spheres, but, if their sport is affected, they will want to know why.

Hain's activities deprived South Africa of tours by MCC and the British Lions. He also brought the problem to the surface with such effect that, I believe, other countries were influenced and South Africa was subsequently outlawed from the Olympic Games.

The repercussions of these events rebounded to and fro within South Africa. Alarm and despondency gradually gave way to a determination to make the bans as short-lived as possible. Before long, many people were working furiously to rid the country's sport of apartheid.

Progress was inevitably slow, but it was at least visible. The abolition of separate entrances and segregated enclosures in the grounds was a major breakthrough, but the biggest was the more recent move which effectively smashed down the barriers and admitted blacks and coloureds into the sporting framework.

The introduction of multi-racial sport perhaps achieved less publicity around the world than those in South Africa would have wanted, for it was a momentous step towards acceptance by the outside world.

It was also a step that would probably not have been considered but for the interference of Hain's group which robbed South Africans of so much international competition at a time when their stock as a sporting nation was reaching a peak.

Maybe I would have felt more bitter if I had been in the position of cricketers such as Mike Procter and Barry Richards, who saw honours and incentive stripped from them almost before they had started on the path to inevitable greatness. But I have been able to view the happenings more objectively than those left inside the country.

The problems are still enormous, for however much is achieved by sporting administrators, the rest of the world cannot ignore the continuing conflicts arising in the day-to-day life of South Africa. Improvements have been made, but it could never be said that the country as a whole accepts all races as equal, which their sport now claims to do.

In justifying my support for Hain, however, I went on to say that South Africa now needed encouragement. Prolonged isolation would only have the effect of persuading the people that their efforts were useless. They would then become resentful and introverted, concerned only with protecting their personal interests. The purpose of the entire campaign would be completely lost.

I believed then, and still do today, that an international team of some sort should undertake a tour of South Africa. Whether it is England going there to play cricket or New Zealand going there for rugby is really irrelevant. They have been in solitary confinement for long enough – the time is ripe for another honest appraisal of their efforts.

Sporting officials from around the world should be present to witness the tour, observe the improvements. Then it would be for them to decide whether attitudes have changed sufficiently for a return to an international schedule, or whether new demands should be made on South Africa. Happily there seems to be a willingness to reappraise the South African sporting scene.

Although this debate took place some years ago, little has changed in overseas attitudes. My views are certainly the same and, with the full-scale introduction of multi-racial competition, the need for a cricket tour of some kind is now even more urgent.

The debate ended amicably enough, and the English newspapers reported my comments very fairly. Unfortunately, the story became distorted on its way to South Africa and I was sent a cutting from an Afrikaans paper carrying the headline : 'Greig working with Hain against South Africa'. It was a disappointing and completely untrue reaction for, to this day, I have still never met Peter Hain.

Whenever I go back to South Africa nowadays, I can guarantee that someone will congratulate me on my foresight in getting out when I did and qualifying for England. I suppose the assumption that it happened that way is understandable, although completely false. Others in South Africa still see me as a traitor.

I have already related how I came to England simply to fill

in a year before beginning my university course and, throughout the early years with Sussex, it never occurred to me that I might be serving some sort of apprenticeship to change cricketing nationalities.

It was Billy Griffith who told me. I was nearing the end of my third season with Sussex when he asked me if I realized that I only needed to play for one more year to be eligible for England.

Surprise though it was, I still didn't take the information very seriously because I knew I wasn't good enough.

Even after I had been picked for England, I put all thoughts of captaining the country out of my mind because I was secretly convinced that my South African background would mitigate against me. I still believe I only got the captaincy because there was no one else in contention. If there had been, the Lord's authorities would have been diplomatic and protected themselves by appointing him rather than me – and I would not have uttered a word of complaint.

As I improved my standing in English cricket, I received the odd nasty letter advising me in firm terms to go back where I had come from. It was something I learned to live with and ignore, just like the abusive cat-calls that have greeted me on many grounds around the country.

There was a sudden increase in my 'fan mail', however, when I committed the biggest blunder of my spell as England captain and told millions of television viewers that I wanted to make the 1976 West Indians grovel.

The implications behind the word did not occur to me at all during the interview. In fact, it wasn't until I picked up the papers the following morning that I realized unhappily what a bad choice 'grovel' had been. My father, rather irately, asked if I had a dictionary at home.

The BBC had shown the interview on the Wednesday evening, prior to the start of the first Test, and the reaction had been strong and immediate. The press picked up the word and blazed it across the top of their Test previews . . . and the inference behind their stories was obvious.

I was painted as a white South African villain ordering black West Indians to grovel before him. My point in using the word had in fact been entirely unconnected with race – I might just as easily have used it while talking about any other side, black or white – but there were many people unwilling to accept my excuse.

All I had intended to convey during the interview was that there were two teams due to play in the Test series, a fact that it had been easy to overlook during the early weeks of the season.

The English press seemed to me to have gone out of their way to build up the West Indians and completely write off our chances. I was annoyed by this approach and, in my enthusiasm to drum up some support for England, I simply used an unfortunate word.

Anonymous letters followed quickly and I had expected nothing else. The anti-South African feeling mounted against me in certain quarters and it took some people a very long time to forgive me.

My position was not helped by the fact that we failed abysmally to force anything like a grovel from a fine West Indian team, and lost 3–0.

9
Early Tests

According to the edict of his father Sandy, Tony had been given until the end of 1970 to make the grade as a top-class cricketer. Neither father nor son had ever forgotten the four-year limit that Sandy had given Tony when Sussex first offered him a contract in 1967 and there is little doubt that Greig senior would have followed his threat through and persuaded Tony to find another job. In 1970, however, the Rest of the World brought their glittering talents to England as a replacement for the cancelled visit of South Africa – and won the first Test by an innings. England made five changes for the second match, at Nottingham, and included in the newcomers was A. W. Greig.

This was it. The childhood dream had materialized, and I was to play for England. Yet it was not exactly with light heart and carefree spirit that I tackled my début at Nottingham. Two things were bothering me and the first was the knowledge that I was quite unprepared for such an honour.

There is no doubt at all in my mind that I simply was not good enough to play for England in 1970. My credentials were three seasons of moderate success in county cricket and the transition to the highest standard of international competition was one that I could well have done without at that point.

My second worry flowed from an undercurrent of resentment which was directed at me and might have been found anywhere from the south coast to Yorkshire.

Here I was, a 23-year-old upstart with a broad South African accent, taking a place in the England side which many believed I was not entitled to.

It was the English authorities who had elected to give me a chance, and by doing so they earned my admiration. It would have been very easy for them to ignore me and avoid the risk of inflating the anti-South Africa balloon. But they stuck by the rules, acknowledged that I was eligible through residence and the birthplace of my father, and decided that I was worth a try, knowing even as they pencilled in my name that it was a controversial selection.

Their confidence in me renewed my yearning to justify my presence in the side and make it impossible for them to leave me out. I wanted to silence the critics who, I was well aware, were hovering around and hoping that I would mess it all up.

My first day was my most successful. Brought on as second change to follow John Snow, David Brown and Basil D'Oliveira, I quickly had Rohan Kanhai caught by Keith Fletcher at slip.

Dolly picked up Graeme Pollock for just two, but the initiative seemed to be slipping away again as Barry Richards and Clive Lloyd shared a half-century stand and took the total to 106 for three.

My brief glory began with the wicket of Richards, caught down the leg side by Alan Knott. Twenty runs later I was celebrating the treasured wicket of Gary Sobers, who had dragged a wide one on to his stumps, and at the same score I added Farokh Engineer to my bag. The World were 126 for six and I had four for not many.

We went on to win that match by eight wickets and, although I only scored 14 runs, I finished with seven wickets – Richards and Sobers again, and Eddie Barlow, making up my second-innings trio.

It was a satisfying start, particularly as we won so handsomely, but I couldn't shake off the impression that I shouldn't really have been there. Even when I took the four wickets, I could almost hear cries of 'Lucky Greig' going up around the doubters as Sobers got out to an uncharacteristic error.

Perhaps I allowed it to affect me too much. Perhaps, which is more likely, I was just not ready for it. Whatever the reason, I had little else to cheer me. By the time we had been beaten at Birmingham and Leeds, I had contributed only 96 runs in five innings, and my wickets total had only crept up to 11.

I can't say I was surprised to be left out of the last Test at The Oval. I consoled myself with the thought that I had, at least, achieved a major ambition and played for England. The authorities later produced an odd ruling and decided that this series was unofficial – though England can seldom, if ever, have faced stronger opposition – but by that time my England cap was already on show. They could never take that away.

One man who came in, as the selectors reshuffled once more for the Oval match, was Lancashire's Peter Lever, a fast bowler who had developed late in his career and was now winning his first cap at almost 30. His inclusion caused an amusing incident at Blackpool, where Sussex met Lancashire during the course of the Test.

Lever was involved in a close race with Sussex seamer Tony Buss to be the first man to take 100 wickets – and the incentive was greater than usual as there was the promise of a sponsored Ford Capri for the winner.

Sussex batted first at Blackpool and I remember we were dismissed for less than 200 on the first day. Down at The Oval, Ray Illingworth won the toss and batted first on Tuesday morning, condemning Lever to the pavilion while Tony Buss enjoyed a long bowling spell on the second day at Blackpool.

I say long spell without a hint of exaggeration. Tony bowled throughout the innings as Lancashire piled up more than 400, and finally claimed the fourth wicket he needed for his hundred, while in a state of near exhaustion.

The victim was Lever's county captain Jack Bond. Peter Graves completed the catch, threw the ball up and started running, pursued by Tony, who seemed to have discovered new energies with the realization that the prize was his. While bewildered spectators and hysterical players looked on, Buss chased Graves all around the Blackpool ground before engulfing him in a triumphant hug.

Ironically, the prize car could so easily have gone north, because Lever opened his Test career with a seven-wicket haul on the Saturday and achieved his own 100 victims.

The MCC squad to tour Australia that winter was chosen immediately after the Oval Test, and I remember sitting in front of the television with Donna as the names in the party were flashed on the screen. Mine was not among them.

I still count my omission from that team as the biggest single disappointment in my career, for the tour was a magnificent English triumph under the masterful captaincy of Illingworth.

Not that my substitute winter was uneventful. I coached at Grahamstown, played for Eastern Province in the Currie Cup – marking my début with that dramatic epileptic attack – and married Donna in Queenstown in March. When I returned to England it was to more disappointment. Richard Hutton of York-shire retained the England all-rounder's position throughout the summer and performed capably.

With a lingering sensation of resignation, I prepared myself for another winter of coaching schoolboys in South Africa. I had got as far as travelling out there and beginning the term when a phone call from England altered all my plans.

It was Donald Carr, secretary of the Test and County Cricket Board, enquiring if I would be available to tour Australia with a Rest of the World team captained by Sobers.

The invitation was a surprise, even when I discovered that a number of earlier choices, Procter among them, had withdrawn. Sobers had put my name forward, conscious as ever of the all-rounder pursuing his own incomparable talent.

Alan Mansell, one of the Sussex youngsters, was flown out to complete my coaching job, and it was agreed that I would travel to Australia with Hylton Ackerman, the South African who had been my contemporary at school and was at that stage playing for Northants.

My father saw the tour as my greatest opportunity, on hard Australian wickets that should suit my aggressive style. I needed no telling that, in his eyes at least, it was almost my last chance to prove that I could sustain a place in the top bracket of world cricket. I had already been selected and then dropped by England and, if I didn't make it this time, I would be under pressure to give up the game and find what Dad would have called 'a proper job'.

I can scarcely imagine a worse start to a tour than I experi-enced when Hylton and I arrived in Adelaide.

My family had seen me off from South Africa, and my father's final pep talk had included lengthy advice that I should listen to every word spoken by the man behind the tour, who just happened to be Sir Donald Bradman.

Who said this was a cissy's game? Waiting to go to hospital after a shot from Stewart Storey broke and disfigured my finger at the Oval in 1970

. . . a sad day – a last look at Brighton beach with Mark before we left England for ever

Opposite above: The three people who matter more to me than anything else in the world – Mark, Donna and Samantha

Opposite below: A happy day, with a kiss from Donna after being named England captain . . .

Doing battle on the school rugby ground stood me in good stead

John Snow and I wearing coloured kit long before World Series

There could never be a better wicket keeper, batsman and friend than Alan Knott

Conversations . . . with a fellow England captain, soccer star Alan Ball

. . . with Ray Illingworth, who should have captained England for longer than he did

. . . with Ian Chappell, tough campaigner, magnificent captain – and arch-enemy number one

Ian Botham – the greatest
all-rounder in the world today

Mike Brearley – a very able
and loyal vice-captain to me

Pointing Doug Walters on his way to the pavilion during MCC's
1974–5 Australian tour

I enjoyed that! Cover-driving during a one day international, 1977

Jubilant with success – a vital part of the make-up, because there are plenty of hard times

Fun at Melbourne – and the Aussie crowds did not know
whether to boo or cheer me

Bondi Beach – just around the corner now

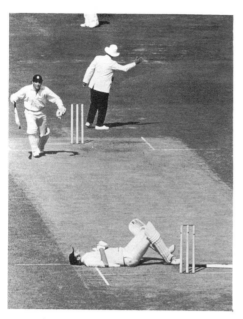

A fire cracker went off and I pretended I'd been shot – the Indians loved it

Chaired in victory by two great team-mates, Chris Old and John Lever

Studying the coin with Bishen Bedi before the potentially crucial toss at Calcutta on the 1976–7 tour

Our unforgettable lap of honour. Will the whole world one day
watch cricket like this?

Derek Underwood, a cricket mate and the best spinner in the world. I was worried that England might not recall him after WSC

The toss before the most exciting Test I have ever played in – the Centenary Test at Melbourne

Catching Richie Robinson, watched by Mike Brearley. By the end of 1977 England were the best fielding outfit in the world – by far

Images of stress. Modelling the first-ever batting crash helmet,
grimacing after losing the toss in Calcutta, and smoking to soothe
the nerves before batting

Willis looks fierce, Knott concerned. McCosker has just had his
jaw broken – Centenary Test, 1977

The most important press conference of my life, confirming the news of WSC. They didn't believe me then, but they do now!

Leaving the High Court with Kerry. Not only did he keep his word to us all, he was tough and soft at the right times, and remains a good friend

Good times. Christmas lunch on tour with wives and families
still frowned upon by some

A very proud moment. Introducing the Queen to my players, 1976

Bradman had been bred into my system from a very early age as I think he even topped Vera Lynn in my father's estimation. The only times that silence was ever demanded in our Queenstown home were when Vera Lynn was singing, the BBC World Service was crackling a Glasgow Rangers soccer commentary on the radio, or Dad was talking about Don Bradman.

I had never met Bradman and it was difficult to imagine his features from the faded photographs I had seen of him. It was a pleasure I was looking forward to as we flew towards Australia.

First stop was Perth, where Hylton and I were met by a group from the local Cricket Lovers' Society. It was midnight, but they took us into the airport buffet for coffee and a chat, which made us feel flattered.

By the time we reached Adelaide we were both itching to catch a glimpse of the real Australia, and the little man in dark glasses and cardigan who approached us as we entered the transit lounge looked just the sort we had been hoping to avoid.

Sure enough, he came out with the predictable lines, welcoming us to Australia and asking us to join him for a coffee. We were just not in the mood for another Cricket Lovers' ritual, so we gave the little man our bags and nipped into the toilet to think of a way out.

Fortunately, as it transpired, we decided not to be rude, and rejoined our friend for the walk to the coffee bar. Two other guys were sitting at the table which he led us to, but their names meant nothing to us – and as the little chap had only mumbled his name by way of introduction I didn't have a clue who he might be.

Cricket chat developed in the expected fashion as we drank coffee, and the trio certainly seemed to know a thing or two. Turning to the cardigan-clad man on my right, I politely enquired if he had anything to do with cricket in the area.

With a surface smile that must have hidden a playful laugh, he replied that the three of them ran the local scene. Still, it all meant nothing to me – they might, after all, have been talking about the airport cricket club.

At about that point, Sobers bounded through the swing doors and headed straight for the little chap. 'How are you, Sir Donald?' he cried – and I don't think I've ever felt more foolish in my life.

D

Hylton had at least shown enough sense to remain reasonably silent during the chat. I had simply made an ass of myself, yet Bradman took it all with a laugh.

When we arrived in Melbourne, I gave the story to the pressmen who met us. The next morning I easily conjured up a mental picture of my father, up early and collecting the papers to see how his boy had fared on arrival in Australia, only to be stunned by the 'Greig snubs Bradman' headlines. Fortunately, he saw the funny side.

At least my performances pleaded for forgiveness. I had a marvellous trip all round, scoring no centuries but consistently passing 50 in addition to taking wickets regularly.

For my future's sake, one of the most pleasing aspects of the trip was that Richard Hutton and I were vying for one place in the 'Test' teams – and I kept him out throughout the series.

But I believe that venture also did international cricket as a whole a great deal of good. It was a goodwill tour, played seriously but in a splendid spirit, and perhaps the most remarkable thing of all was that Sobers managed to keep his team together.

The world accepted that Sobers was a matchless all-rounder. But, as a captain, he had strong and numerous critics. I can only speak from the experience of one tour, but I would have chosen no one else to lead such a side.

To appreciate the problems he faced it is necessary to know that his squad included players from the West Indies, England, South Africa, India, Pakistan and New Zealand.

The South African situation alone could have been explosive enough, but, to make things a thousand times more delicate, war broke out between India and Pakistan during the course of our tour. Somehow, the spirit of the team never faltered, and Sobers must take a large part of the credit for that.

He could at times be deceptively casual, almost lazy in his attitudes, but there was never any doubt who was in control. He was in constant demand for public appearances, autographs, match tickets and a hundred other chores, but he managed it all capably, choosing the golf course and his beloved clubs as his escape route.

If I needed further proof of his greatness, he provided it during the Melbourne Test, in which we had made an abysmal start.

We sat together in a bedroom one night with defeat seemingly a dawn away. Sobers refused to abandon hope and I shall never forget the promise he made to me. 'If I have to do it all by myself,' he said, 'I shall make sure we win this match.'

By close of play the next evening, Sobers had scored 130 not out, well on his way to an innings of 254 that no less an authority than Bradman rated the finest he had ever seen.

It was an extraordinary innings that merits the much-used adjective brilliant more than anything else I have been part of in cricket. It was almost blinding in its power. We feared every ball that he would be out, because it seemed just too good to go on. But go on it did, and Sobers' late-night promise over a drink had not been forgotten.

That tour gave me experience that was to prove vital. It gave me confidence, developed my technique and my temperament. When I flew home, I felt at last that I was ready for the demands of Test cricket. I also felt that I must have done enough in Australia to merit an England place in the Ashes series that summer, and so it was to prove.

I went into the team for the first Test at Manchester and, between then and the end of the Ashes series in England five years later, I was to complete an unbroken sequence of fifty-eight Test appearances.

It was to my advantage that Australia provided the opposition in 1972 as I had recent first-hand information on all their players. As with most Australian teams, they arrived in England with the critics already writing them off as the worst ever. I knew differently, for they had two opening bowlers, both new to England, who were to make a remarkable impact on the series.

Dennis Lillee is another story; his greatest days and our memorable contests were yet to come. But Bob Massie is a name that should awaken a few rusty memories.

Any bowler who can consistently baffle Gary Sobers wins my vote as a star, and that is just what Massie had done during the World tour. Sobers never tried to pick seam or swing, preferring always to use his remarkable eye to play it as it came. But Massie had him puzzled.

A couple of inswingers to the left-hander would be followed by an outswinger, without any detectable change in action. Massie had Sobers caught in the slip cordon more than once and, apart from at Melbourne, worried him in almost every innings.

Coupled with the already fearsome pace of Lillee, these two posed a danger that I was quick to point out to my new team-mates when I arrived at Manchester for the opening battle in the series.

As it turned out, they made little impression at Old Trafford. England won comfortably and I started well with two half-centuries and five wickets. But the memory of the match that I have always carried is of the number of catches we dropped.

For some reason which I can't now recall, we turned up for nets on the Wednesday without a specialist slip fielder in the side. I was the closest as I fielded there part-time for Sussex, but we were in desperate need of a reliable first-slip catcher.

Ray Illingworth called us together and asked for volunteers and John Snow surprised us all by putting up his hand. 'Snowy' was obviously keen to get away from the third-man boundary, where he was generally banished between bowling spells, so Illingworth included him in the cordon as we got down to some catching practice.

As the captain deflected balls into the slips at varying heights and pace, Snowy caught some blinders, mostly by sticking out a hand in that inimitably casual way of his.

There seemed little alternative, so Illingworth decided to field Snow at first slip, and we lined up for Geoff Arnold's opening spell the following morning with Snow, Greig and Illingworth as the three slips.

It was a typical Manchester morning, cold, grey and damp, with enough green in the wicket to make Arnold's eyes light up. These were the conditions he prayed for, and I felt for him as Snowy and I managed to spill three catches from consecutive balls in one of the most amazing chapters of bungling I've ever seen.

The first one flew head-high to first slip and, as I turned to watch, Snow was a floundering mass of arms and hair. He got a despairing hand on the ball, but could only deflect it to third man for four.

I dropped the next one, a sitter at comfortable height for which I had no excuse. Snowy had by now adjusted his stance, standing more upright to cope with the sort of flying edge which had just defeated him. It was fitting in our state of confusion that the next ball fizzed low off the outside edge and hit him on the ankle.

Illingworth fumed until I thought he might explode, and Snow was hustled back to the outfield after one of the shortest-ever careers at slip.

Later in the day I put another one down, this time off Basil D'Oliveira, and the one I did manage to hang on to was taken at full stretch to my left, right in front of a surprised Brian Luckhurst, Snowy's deputy.

At each interval, the roasting from Illingworth grew in ferocity and, as the close drew near, I think every member of the close catchers had dropped at least one – except the captain.

Our salvation arrived with a nick to third slip, which hit Ray firmly on the chest and flopped to the turf. Minutes later, play was over for the day and Ray went straight on television to complain that Old Trafford was the worst ground for sighting the ball he had ever played on!

Australia levelled the rubber at 1–1 with a handsome win at Lord's which owed almost everything to the efforts of Bob Massie. By taking seventeen wickets in the match and bending the ball fantastically, he convinced me that he is the finest exponent of medium-paced swing bowling I've ever faced, and convinced a number of cynics that he must be using the prohibited grease substance, lip-ice, on the ball.

I don't know why it is, but every time a bowler succeeds in his aim and produces significant swing, he is accused of cheating. It happened to England's John Lever in India in 1977, when the home captain Bishen Bedi suggested that he was coating the ball with vaseline. That allegation was as groundless and degrading as, I'm sure, were those directed at Massie.

Similar snipes are often aimed at young fast bowlers. During the Ashes series of 1977, England's Bob Willis and Australia's Len Pascoe were both accused of chucking. Most of the time, those who accuse are either making excuses for the failure of their own team, or seeking sensational publicity for themselves.

Massie's efforts at Lord's should enter the same category as Jim Laker's capture of nineteen Australian wickets at Manchester in 1956. Laker was bowling on a raging turner, ideal for his off-spin, but Massie was producing his own brand of magic purely through the air, without any need for help from the pitch conditions.

Laker's legend lives on, and deservedly so. But how many people remember Bob Massie now?

He was a nice, quiet guy who had the ability to make the ball perform. He did it naturally, and it was almost impossible for the batsman to differentiate between the one that left him and the one that dipped in late.

Eventually, one of the daily papers produced a series of photographs which, they claimed, illustrated that there was a noticeable difference in action. I believe it was this revelation, more than anything else, which put Massie on the way back to obscurity.

He suddenly began to think obsessively about his bowling and allow himself to become overwhelmed by theories. When he returned to Australia he had lost it all and, if you try to find him playing now, look first around the junior club sides.

The Third Test at Nottingham was the one draw in the series, and England guaranteed the retention of The Ashes by destroying Australia inside three days at Headingley.

This was Derek Underwood's triumph – another near-unplayable spell on a wet wicket – but John Snow constantly reminds me that he also made an unusual number of runs, lapping, if I remember rightly, almost every ball.

By now I was learning fast that the Tests against Australia were the only ones that really mattered to many Englishmen. I was caught up in the patriotism of it all and it was a real pleasure to go into the Aussies' travelling marquee on that Saturday evening at Leeds and drink their beer with the Ashes in our grasp.

Cricket was now my life to an extent where it was hard to imagine myself ever doing anything else. The following winter's tour of India did nothing to lessen the passion.

It was the first MCC tour to India for some years and was to be a trip of vital importance to me when I returned as England captain four years later.

This was the winter in which I fell in love with the Indian crowds and they, in turn, seemed to fall for me. By the time we had played the second Test in Calcutta's enormous Eden Gardens stadium, I felt like a star of show business.

The Indians have a passion for cricket that is difficult to explain to anyone who has not physically experienced it. They are noisy, uninhibited, fiercely partisan. Yet they will attach their affections to a visiting team or player just as easily.

We were a popular team, under the careful and intelligent captaincy of Tony Lewis, and my blond hair and unusual height endeared me immediately to the crowds.

For the first time in my career I found myself playing up to the fans, clowning in the field and making them laugh. It's not something I would ever attempt in Australia, and I often think twice about it in England. But in India, make them laugh and you are their hero, just as Derek Randall discovered on the 1976–7 trip.

By Christmas we were 1–0 up, having won at Delhi in very satisfying fashion, Tony Lewis and I knocking off the winning runs. But we were narrowly beaten at Calcutta, and hammered in the heat of Madras.

The last two Tests were drawn to give India victory in the series, but I was able to strike another personal ambition from my list by scoring my first Test hundred – 148 at Bombay.

Batting against the best spinners was an aspect of my game that had needed a great deal of work. I had always tended to lunge at the turning ball, often overbalancing in the process, but in India you cannot afford that sort of vulnerability – you learn or fail. I learned, thanks chiefly to the advice and assistance of men like Keith Fletcher, a wonderful player against the slow men.

It was fitting that my first century was scored in a partnership with 'Fletch', who also reached three figures himself. And, although the match was drawn and the series lost, the baying of the crowd called us back and Lewis led us around the Brabourne Stadium on an unforgettable lap of honour.

That century had been enough to ensure me the 'Man of the Series' award, but the tour dragged on a little longer for me – all the way back to the dark corridors of Lord's and a disciplinary hearing.

Cricketers visiting India need to employ considerable powers of self-discipline to cope with the peculiar problems of pitches, crowds, climate, diet and umpires which combine to produce a pressure more severe than in any other cricketing country. On that tour in 1972–3 I allowed myself to over-react and I was rightly carpeted for it.

Donald Carr, the tour manager, had to speak to me during the Calcutta Test for a spot of time-wasting, but the worst episode came later in the series, when India's captain Ajit Wadekar was given 'in' after I had caught him knee-high at slip.

Several of our lads showed a degree of anger, but for me it was just too much. I raced down the pitch, brandishing the ball above my head and shrieking at the umpire. The decision was eventually reversed and Wadekar had to go, but, however effective the tactics of complaint had been, I knew I was wrong and I accepted the rebuke from the manager.

I was summoned to Lord's as soon as we returned home and told politely but firmly that success on the field can never excuse gamesmanship or dissent.

It was a temperamental stage of my life, in which I probably needed a measure of responsibility to occupy me. I found it sooner than expected, because Sussex offered me the captaincy for the 1973 season.

10

Tours and traumas

Sussex were in a rut. Throughout the late sixties and early seventies, they had languished around the foot of the County Championship, cheered only by intermittent success in the Gillette Cup. Worse, they became known around the country as a discontented, disorganized club. Mike Griffith, who many thought should never have been captain anyway, wilted under the growing pressure, but the fault was not exclusively his. When Greig was appointed county captain, he was faced with rebuilding the team and helping to restructure the much-criticized committee. For the first time in his career, he was obliged to involve himself in the politics, petty and otherwise, within his club. He had to do it at a time when his England career was threatening to make him a household name.

I had to make it plain from the start that those expecting instant miracles were living in the wrong world. Sussex had been struggling for a number of years and, in my first statement as the new captain, I spelled out that it must necessarily take quite a long time to re-establish the county as a force in England.

We didn't just have to work on the youngsters – we had to find them first! Things had been allowed to drift to such an extent that it was difficult to see any young talent readily available.

Sussex had even managed to blunder in the overseas market. When I took over, our two imports were Geoff Greenidge, the Barbadian opener, and Uday Joshi, a little-known Indian spinner. Two nicer chaps you could not have wished to meet, but they would have been the first to confess that they rated pretty low in any international talent list.

On one side of us, Hampshire boasted Barry Richards, Gordon Greenidge and Andy Roberts. On the other, Kent included Asif Iqbal, Bernard Julien and John Shepherd. Our two signings just weren't in the same class and it was one of my main priorities to sort out this situation and ensure that any future signings from overseas were given more thought.

The county had always been important to me, but until 1973 I had been able to play purely a player's part. Now I needed not only to concern myself with the team, but also with affairs of the committee and the members.

It was no secret at that time that many other counties thought of us as an unhappy club – and maybe they were right. Success breeds contentment and we had enjoyed precious little of that, but there was more to it than a simple shortage of talent. There were many things to be put right behind the scenes, as I soon discovered when I set myself to my first objective – making Sussex a better place to play cricket.

Gradually, things changed and Hove became a happier and more ambitious base. My main aim as skipper remained unfulfilled – we did not win a major competition. But the staff became stronger, the spirit immeasurably better, and there is no way I could have achieved even this without the unflinching assistance of such great club men as the Buss brothers, who seem to crop up in my story so frequently.

Ironically, we might have won something in my first year as captain – a year in which I chose to stand back and make objective observations rather than charge in with proposals for sweeping changes.

Rather unexpectedly, we won our way through to Lord's for the Gillette Cup Final against Gloucestershire. We had no particular right to be there, because we were not, in truth, a very good side. But the lure of the Gillette has always, in my experience, stimulated the entire Sussex staff down to Jim the dressing-room attendant. The adrenalin flows, nerve-ends are exposed and the spirit soars at the very mention of that razor company.

We put up a brave fight before surrendering, and had a laugh on the way. Roger Marshall, our lanky ginger-haired seam bowler known to all as 'Bluey', had never played at Lord's before and, when his turn to bat arrived, he was nothing but a bundle of nerves.

It seemed to the rest of us, sitting watching from the team balcony, that 'Bluey' was taking a remarkably long time to get out on the ground, even allowing for the two flights of stairs one has to descend and the harrowing walk through the crowded Long Room.

When he eventually hurried down the pavilion steps he seemed even more overwrought than when he had left us, but we had to wait until his return for the real explanation. Just as David Steele was to do on his England début two seasons later, 'Bluey' had misjudged the descent, taken one flight of steps too many and found himself hopelessly lost in the Gents'.

Although Tony Brown won the Man of the Match award, I felt Mike Procter had played the most significant role in Gloucestershire's win, and the very presence of Pakistani stars Zaheer Abbas and Sadiq Mohammed in the same side as Procter highlighted once again what we were missing in the way of overseas players.

Our progress to the final, and the consequent euphoria around the county, set me thinking. Why was it just the Gillette Cup which motivated our players? Why couldn't they produce a similar standard of cricket in the other competitions? And why did the crowds only flock to Hove for the Gillette games?

I came up with an answer which simply confirmed my long-standing opinion that English county cricketers are expected to play far too much. Our team was reaching saturation point and, with limited ability, they were only able to raise their game on the odd occasion. The Gillette spurred them because success in that competition was something of a tradition at Sussex, while, in the run-of-the-mill Championship games, the players grew into the habit of almost playing from memory.

People ask why England cannot produce cricketers with the flair of the Australians and West Indians. I suggest there is nothing more mysterious involved than the plain fact that the Australians, the West Indians, and every other cricketing nation come to that, have never tried to cram their seasons so full of fixtures that one could imagine a day without cricket as a national disaster.

Cricket is no different from any other activity, in that if you play it too often you are bound to get stale. Yet in England we seemed to take a masochistic delight in increasing the programme almost every year.

The travelling is as big a factor as the playing in the chiselling away of players' enthusiasm. Weekends during the county season nowadays are something of a sick joke.

A typical weekend could start with the completion of a Championship match at Hove on Friday evening, followed by a drive through the night to reach Manchester in time for a late meal and a night's sleep before the start of a new Championship fixture on Saturday.

At close of play, you pack up again, stow the kit away in the cars and get back on the motorway to Birmingham, venue for Sunday's John Player League match. After an exciting match in front of a big crowd, you scarcely have time to digest a beer before driving back up to Manchester, where Monday morning finds you playing to a soul-destroying lack of spectators, while physically and mentally exhausted . . . in short, far from the ideal frame of mind in which to tackle a Championship match.

Not all weekends are that hectic, but some are considerably worse and, until something is done to cut back the amount of travelling involved in the English season, I don't think any of us can be surprised that the likes of Greg Chappell and Viv Richards seldom emerge in England.

Unless some formula can be found by which the professional game is worth more money – so that prospective stars are drawn in – and involves less fatigue – so that they are not very quickly persuaded out again – I believe the day will come when the full-time system that we now know is phased out completely.

Australia survives very nicely without any seven-days-a-week professionals and, for the life of me, I can't see why England should not do the same.

I appreciate that it will require a substantial amount of restructuring and send most of the present-day county clubs into extinction. But, on the other hand, an Australian-style graded system with weekend cricket and, maybe, a midweek inter-city league with eight four-day games every season for each city club, has innumerable advantages.

The greatest of the plus-marks would be that English cricket would no longer outlaw doctors, lawyers, journalists and men in a hundred and one other professions simply because they could not afford to take the risk of throwing away their profitable career and turning to a full-time cricket alternative that carries no guarantee of long-term security.

How many potential Test players England may have missed by creating a county system with such restrictions is impossible to estimate. But in these times when the commercial market is so open for top sports stars, I feel it would make sense to prune the first-class programme to a level where no one need be exempt.

My views are not held universally, even by cricketers, and one who has very different opinions is the man who played the 'victim's' part in 1973's biggest cricket story, Ray Illingworth.

While beginning my spell as captain of Sussex, I also continued to be a part of the England team which, in 1973, beat New Zealand but lost to the West Indies in a twin-tour summer.

At the end of it, supposedly under the pretext of the West Indies defeat, Illingworth was sacked as England captain. It was a move which enraged a lot of people and, I have to admit, left me quite bewildered.

Illingworth is the best tactical captain I have ever played under – although Mike Brearley now runs him very close – and his three years as captain had brought England a good deal of success.

The authorities may have had an ulterior motive for wanting him out. If they had, I know nothing of it. On the surface, it seemed a surprising decision and I believe to this day that it was a very premature dismissal.

I bear no personal grudge against Mike Denness, the man who replaced Ray for the winter tour of the West Indies. Mike is a nice fellow and a good cricketer, but his Test experience was very limited. He had been vice-captain to Tony Lewis on the previous winter's Indian tour, but had achieved no great success with the bat and took the job with many critics arguing that he was not worth a place in the team.

From the outset it was a torrid tour – a great pity, because it was my first visit to the West Indies and I thoroughly enjoyed most of the islands. We were soundly beaten in the First Test, and I will never know how we managed to stay in the series at only 1–0 down right up to the final match at Port of Spain.

Frankly, we were not in the same class as the West Indies, who were growing into a formidable combination. And poor Denness did not ease his problems by having a wretched time with the bat.

Slightly to my surprise I had been appointed tour vice-captain, so it was essential that I remained as loyal to Denness as possible. The responsibility involved me in one or two unpleasant duties, the most memorable of which was a clash with Geoff Boycott.

When Illingworth was sacked, Boycott was many people's choice as the natural successor. He knew it and, with the dedication that has stamped every step of his extraordinary career, I believe he prepared himself to accept it. I can appreciate that it must have jolted him quite severely when the job went to Denness, and, unfortunately, he did not easily forget.

A number of the other senior players on the trip had also been against the appointment, which resulted in an undesirable split in the camp. But my major problem was to alleviate the difficulty caused by the moods and attitudes of Boycott, and I was determined to confront him with my complaints.

It was an odd situation really. At 27, I still had less than two full years of Test cricket behind me, yet here I was feeling the need to tick off a man six years and more than forty Tests my senior, whom I had first watched playing for England in 1964 while I was still at school in South Africa.

He heard me out, then put some pretty forcible points of his own and the discussion caused a rift between us lasting more than a week, in which we never once exchanged words.

The situation was saved by the fact that Donna, my wife, and Anne, a friend of Geoff's, were both on the tour with us at that stage. Unknown to either Geoff or myself, they formulated a plan that would mean the four of us having dinner together one night in the hotel. It wasn't an immediate success and I remember the two of us glaring at each other for a while, but common sense prevailed, the argument was put behind us and we struck up an altogether better relationship.

I wish I could claim to have won him round completely, but within months of this incident, Geoff announced that he was no longer available for England and proceeded to take himself into a three-year exile, broken so triumphantly in 1977.

At least it did help us through the tour, however. Geoff threw himself into practices with much more spirit and the morale of the side improved under his direction.

Then, almost unbelievably, we levelled the series at Port of Spain. Geoff scored a century in one innings and 90 in the other and I employed off-spin to take thirteen wickets.

I had learned very early in the tour that there is no future in bowling medium-pace seamers on West Indian wickets. Clive Lloyd taught me that lesson rather painfully and I soon tired of seeing his right foot plunge down the pitch and the ball disappear out of the ground.

The wickets favour the batsmen so much that you need to bowl either speed or spin to have a chance, which is why so few medium-pacers ever play for the West Indies.

We were up against a fair number of left-handers on that trip, so I worked on developing round-the-wicket off-spin. The first time I tried it out, I took six wickets in Barbados, but that was relative failure compared to Port of Spain.

I have never bowled better than in that Test, either before or since. Everything was right – the run-up, the loop in flight and the length. Apart from the thrill of contributing to the result which squared the series, it was very satisfying to prove myself more versatile than some people believed.

On an ironic note, Boycott's success with the bat, just as influential in our win, ensured that Denness kept the captaincy for the English summer when another defeat might have made life harder for him.

The summer Tests against India and Pakistan did not threaten Denness's position – even though Pakistan managed to win the series – and it was no surprise when he was named to lead MCC to Australia the following winter.

It was, however, a personal disappointment that I was discarded as vice-captain in favour of John Edrich, who had not been available for the West Indies trip. Edrich was a player of vast experience and I could have no real quarrel with the decision. But I was left wondering why, on that basis, Boycott had not been Denness's deputy the previous winter. . . .

This time there was no Boycott. No John Snow either, which certainly didn't help our chances. But great players though these two are, I don't think their presence in Australia that winter would have made any difference at all to the outcome.

Australia walloped us, and the reason was that Dennis Lillee recovered full fitness sooner than expected and a formidable pace partner was uncovered for him in the shape of Jeff Thomson.

On the way out, however, we knew nothing of these developments. Lillee, as far as we knew, was still laid up with the back injury that threatened to end his career – and without wishing him further harm we probably all hoped he would stay there for a few more months. And Thomson? He was just a beach boy who had played one Test against Pakistan in 1972–3 and come away with nought for 110. Why should he worry us?

Having suffered the blow of losing the vice-captaincy, my pride was partially restored when Alec Bedser, the tour manager, approached me on the plane and asked me to be on the selection committee. I agreed readily, never thinking that so much soul-searching was to go into that committee before the tour was over.

The first indication that things were not going to be easy came with the news that Lillee was back in action. We saw him bowl off a short run-up at Perth, and I remember admiring his courage and dedication for fighting back from the sort of injury that would have finished many players.

There was a general buzz around the country over Thomson and the Australian press, in their normal fashion, built up their own side and predicted an almighty hammering for the English.

To find out more about the mysterious Thomson, I consulted Bruce Francis, the Australian opener who had spent some time playing for Essex. He confirmed that Thommo was very rapid and added that the most disconcerting aspect of his bowling was that he hadn't the slightest idea where the ball was going.

Thomson and Lillee were named as the opening bowlers in Australia's First Test team at Brisbane and it wasn't long before I had guaranteed myself a slice of the action.

Lillee was batting and had scored about 15 against some gentle stuff from our fast men. I had seen enough of this and decided that if the 'fast bowlers' union' prevented *them* from bouncing Lillee, *I* would do it for them. Mike Denness gave me a bowl on request and my first delivery reared at Lillee's head, flicking his glove and giving Alan Knott a simple catch.

There are those who still insist that it was that single delivery from me that sparked off the bouncer war to follow. I reject the theory totally and refuse to accept that it made the slightest bit of difference. What it had done, though, was to rile Lillee, and as he passed me on his stalking path back to the pavilion he uttered enough words to let me know that my turn would come.

It came sooner than I would have wished, because Lillee and Thomson were not slow to sort out our early batsmen. We were in real trouble when I went out to bat, and the sight of Lillee pawing the turf at the end of an enormous run was enough to send the crowd into a frenzy of anticipation.

Lillee had not forgotten his threats and he proceeded to try and kill me. The first ball flashed past my nose, gathered height to clear the leap of wicket-keeper Rod Marsh and hit the sightscreen first bounce. Nor did it end there. I continued to play up to him and, the more upset he became, the worse he bowled, for Brisbane was a sporty wicket on which the ball of fuller length was the danger delivery.

I began to exaggerate my follow-through and signal my own fours, well aware that his rage would do nothing to help his length or direction. I reached a century with the aid of a good deal of luck, but the innings remains as memorable as any I have ever played, partly because it was my first hundred against Australia, partly because it had been a century in a crisis, but most of all because it was scored against the finest fast-bowling combination I have ever faced.

Thomson had worried me from the start. He got past the outside edge three times in his first over at me, and, whether he knew where they were going or not, they were all very fine deliveries.

At the end of that over, I sauntered down the pitch for a chat with John Edrich and asked him to take Thomson until I got myself settled. Edrich agreed with the most unexpected proviso I could have imagined. He would look after Thomson, he explained, as long as I agreed to farm the strike if Terry Jenner was brought on.

Jenner was one of the friendliest leg-spinners in Test cricket, and Edrich's request seemed to me comparable with asking a man if he would eat a steak when he had been starved for a week. I didn't argue.

The agreement backfired in any case, for, in helping me out, Edrich had his wrist broken by Thomson, one of many injuries we were to suffer on our careworn struggles around the country.

Later in that innings I was joined at the wicket by Derek Underwood, one of the bravest tail-end batsmen I have ever seen. He came towards me for the customary mid-wicket chat and asked if I had any advice. 'Yes,' I replied. 'Fight for your life.' With a look that was half-amused and half-alarmed, 'Deadly' returned to the striker's end. His second ball from Thomson was a fierce bouncer, and Derek took off in that often-photographed pose of his, both feet off the ground, head turned away and bat brandished in baseball fashion.

As the ball seared under the elbow he had thrown in front of his face, missing his ear by inches, Derek's placid expression turned into a look of horror. At the end of the over he came back down the wicket and said simply: 'I see what you mean.'

Both Lillee and Thomson were wonderful pace bowlers in their own right. The short-pitched ball was just one of their weapons, but on that tour it was certainly the most effective. No batsman likes having to duck and weave to protect his life, and most of us experimented with different systems to combat the threat.

Fred Titmus thought he had found the answer. His plan involved taking guard on leg stump and adopting a stance with his feet nine to twelve inches outside. He was an obvious target for the short ball slanting down the leg-side, but Fred was ready for it. Each time he saw the bumper leave the bowler's hand, he would literally jump across the stumps, landing outside off stump while the ball passed safely over his back.

One morning he was particularly successful, and both Lillee and Thomson were becoming visibly frustrated. I imagine Ian Chappell must have had a word with them during the lunch interval because, almost immediately after the resumption, Lillee released a short one at Fred, aimed outside off stump.

Fred saw it coming too late – he was already in mid-air. He abandoned ship half-way through his jump and, amid a flurry of bat, gloves and cap, somehow managed to avoid the ball. He ended up on his back, however, and never again employed his plan against the bouncer.

It would be easy at this distance for any English batsman to boast that he was never scared during that series. But, if we are truthful, I think all of us experienced fear at some stage.

Up to a point, I believe nerves are essential to success. If I go out to bat feeling completely calm, something is wrong. In fact, I very rarely do. I can sleep in the dressing-room right up to the moment when I am needed at the crease. But it needs only a splash of water over my face and a walk down the pavilion steps to get the adrenalin flowing again.

Fear must never be allowed to dominate, which is why I dislike sitting down to watch the play before I go out. It does me no good to see other batsmen throwing themselves around as the ball flies about their ears, because my innings could be completely different.

What we really needed in Australia that winter was as many experienced batsmen as we could lay hands on – and our resources were steadily dwindling through injuries.

The selection committee eventually decided that a replacement should be called, and I was with the majority in thinking it would be foolish to bring out a youngster to be thrown in against Lillee and Thomson on the fastest, bounciest wicket in the world at Perth.

My choice was Colin Cowdrey, and the grand old man of Kent and England cricket was finally summoned while the Aussies mocked us as 'Dad's Army'.

When the familiar beaming face and rotund figure of Cowdrey joined us, I recall witnessing an amusing ceremony. As Colin released the lock on his cricket case, it sprang open as if alive; then gradually, like bread rising in the oven, a mountain of foam rubber rose from the interior.

This was Cowdrey's protection, and he had obviously been well briefed. He padded almost every part of his body, but nobody laughed – we had seen enough to convince us he was right.

Colin opened for us at Perth, batted a long time and served his purpose. Time after time he would allow the ball to thunder into the thigh pad or his chest protector, for it had only needed a couple of attempts to warn him that hooking was just not on.

Useful as Cowdrey was, nothing could stem the tide, and it had to be faced that Australia were the far better side. Ian Chappell was an inspiring captain, but it is easy to lead when you have a stack of class batsmen and a pace attack that includes Max

Walker and Gary Gilmour in addition to the Lillee–Thomson spearhead.

Mike Denness suffered badly. He had been ill at the start of the tour and he could find no sort of form against the pacemen. Eventually, he showed a courage that demanded admiration and dropped himself for the Sydney Test.

It was the right thing to do at the time, just as it was right that he should return for the last rites in Melbourne. Mike scored a century there and we finished the series with a win. But it must have been as clear to him as it was to the rest of us that his time as England's captain was running short.

I I

England, my England!

The 1975 World Cup came and went with Mike Denness still clinging on to the England leadership. He retained the job for the first of a hurriedly arranged four-Test series against the Australians – and probably wished he hadn't. Denness gambled on putting the Aussies in to bat, and met the subsequent defeat, castigation and sacking in dignified silence. Tony Greig was the choice of public and selectors to take charge.

Believe it or not, it was only when I sat down with the Sunday papers on the rest day of the First Test that I at last began to appreciate how close I might be to becoming England captain.

I had not been blind to the troubles of Mike Denness and I suppose I was conscious of the probability that his future was uncertain in the extreme. But it had never really occurred to me that I would be chosen as his successor.

I still believed that my South African background would count against me and, if and when the job became available, I was prepared to be passed over on those grounds.

It is hard to say how much, at that stage, Mike wanted to go on as captain. He had taken so much punishment from the media that it must have penetrated to him, but he was a man who rarely gave his feelings away.

He had led the side in the World Cup, in which we won all our group matches then went out to Australia in a low-scoring semi-final. It was an invigorating competition to play in and, I imagine, to watch. Naturally, there were teething troubles, but it was a great innovation for cricket and an equally big success when repeated, four years later.

The first sign that the selectors had begun to doubt Denness came with his appointment for only the first of the four Tests

against Australia. It didn't need an interpreter to spell it out then
– this was Mike's last chance to stop the rot.

It is now a well-known piece of cricket history that Denness's
fate was sealed by the toss of a coin. He put them in, we were
ambushed by rain when we batted and beaten by an innings.

In fairness, Mike did ask around the dressing-room before
taking the decision that effectively put his neck on the block. I
advised him that he should bat if in doubt, but that he should also
consult the bowlers.

It would be pointless to mention names here, but I happen to
know that Mike was not alone in his conviction. Several other
England players that morning were in favour of fielding first.

Of course, it is always a gamble to put a side in first, but that
is not to say it is not sometimes a good thing. Mike was desperately
unlucky. The Australians topped 300, unhindered by the weather,
and we had been at the crease for no more than an over when a
thunderstorm drenched the ground.

At that time, Test wickets in England could not be covered
during playing hours – something I always deplored – and it could
be said that that regulation cost Denness his job. Max Walker,
who had laughed out loud at the insanity of leaving the pitch open
to the rain, became almost unplayable and took four of the first
five wickets, including both Denness and myself. Lillee finished us
off for 101 and Thomson bowled us out again.

At the close of the third day, however, we had tottered to 93
for five in our second innings, still the best part of 200 behind.
My part in the match was almost certainly over as Walker had
dismissed me for a second time and, on Sunday lunchtime, most
of us drove out of Birmingham to a countryside pub.

The Sunday papers were lying on a table, and as I opened them
at the cricket page I felt a strong and immediate sympathy for
Denness. Without exception, the Sunday columnists had crucified
him.

A number of them put my name forward as the next captain,
but on that Sunday lunchtime I told myself I would never slide
into the position in which Mike Denness was now languishing. I
would get out before I could be crucified.

I sat in that pub and cast my mind back through previous
England captains I had known – Ray Illingworth, who had won,

then retained the Ashes, oddly sacked after one poor series; Tony Lewis, who had done a splendid, if defeated job with an under-strength side in India, dismissed and scarcely heard of again as a player. There seemed little doubt that the England job was an unpredictable one in which you needed both a share of luck and a good side to survive. Yet I knew I wanted it.

A phone call from Alec Bedser told me of my appointment. By that time, it was unexpected only in the way in which Alec phrased it. 'I have got something I would like to ask you,' he said.

'Oh yes,' I replied.

'Would you accept the captaincy for the rest of the series?' he asked.

I was astonished, not by the appointment but by the fact that it had been put to me as if they thought I might refuse it. Of that, there was naturally no chance.

In the period to follow I was to grow necessarily closer to Alec Bedser and learn to respect and admire him. It was not a perfect relationship by any means – we had our share of differences – but, throughout my time as captain, I was appreciative of the fact that it had been Alec, above anyone else, who had put me there.

It must have been a difficult decision to take, but he stuck by me faithfully. He helped me frequently and I remember him saying often, 'Don't let me down.' I don't think I did let him down, although I thought of him more than anyone else when I made the decision to join Kerry Packer's scheme.

Alec may think I betrayed him at that point. But, although he would not admit it, I am convinced that had he been in my shoes, he would have done exactly as I did.

After his phone call, I prepared myself for the inevitable in-vasion by the media. It was an unforgettable day, hectic in the extreme, but emotional and exciting, too.

Most of the cricket writers came to my home and the papers next morning published very favourable reactions to the appoint-ment. I was pleased and flattered enough to file all the cuttings away, but it wasn't long before the mood of euphoria began to concern me.

Telegrams were arriving from all over the world, the phone scarcely stopped ringing and I couldn't move through a street without being slapped on the back and told 'Things will be different now' or, 'The Aussies won't know what's hit them, eh, Tony?' It was the comments which worried me, because it was becoming increasingly clear that a great number of people expected everything to change simply because England had a new captain.

It was an understandable reaction. We were in an abysmal run and the public wanted to see something new, something different. Maybe I had the personality and the physical appearance which fitted their wish, but it got to the point when I wanted to turn on the well-wishers and ask them what they expected me to do.

Give or take one or two changes, I was to be captaining the same team which had failed under Mike Denness – and I had never pretended to be a great captain when it came to strategy. My qualities have always been concerned with motivating players, making them want to win. But for technical decisions I have generally pooled my resources with my senior players, who, in the case of England, were to become Alan Knott, Keith Fletcher and Mike Brearley.

We did halt the team's slide that summer and draw the last three Tests, which was logically as much as I could have hoped to do. I expected the public to be pleased about it all but, instead, the plight of the captain was hammered into me – they now demanded a victory.

To my mind, we were putting pride back into our game – and we had actually been in control for long periods of the Second and Third Tests. But it seemed this was not good enough; the cynics counted up and announced that I had been captain for three Tests and not achieved a victory. It was an attitude that considerably upset me at the time.

My first team as England captain had shown four changes from the beaten Birmingham side – and only one of them caused any great stir. That was the choice of a 33-year-old uncapped Northamptonshire batsman to come in at number three.

It had by no means been a snap decision to select David Steele. The theory had been in my mind ever since I sat down and tried to formulate my first thoughts as skipper. Then, shortly before the selectors met to pick the side for Lord's, Sussex played at Northampton.

I had dinner one night with Bob Cottam, the Northants seamer who had been with me on my first MCC tour, and he confirmed my opinion. Then I had a chat with David himself and my mind was made up.

It was a selection that was bound to be greeted with a mixture of curiosity and apprehension, maybe even a tinge of derision. But I saw Steele as a fine example of a player who had, for ten years, been longing to win a place in the England side.

He was never the most stylish player and he never will be. But, after his selection was known, David would have gone under a bus for me because I had played a large part in ending his long wait.

I shall never forget the moment when I handed over his cap in the traditional pre-match ceremony in the dressing-room. As I shook David's hand he was literally shaking with emotion and I swear there were tears running down inside his glasses.

Those thick glasses were just part of the make-up that endeared David Steele to the public. The silver-grey hair, hunched walk, intense stare and occasional wide grin all contributed to his rapid progress into the hearts of many people who had previously shown little interest in cricket.

More than anything, though, he won stardom through his performances on the field. He did the job he was picked for better than I could have dared to hope – and, on that first morning at Lord's, we needed every run that his bat could produce.

It was 49 for four when I went in to join Steele and, even as I descended the stairs from the dressing-room, I could see the evening paper placards outside in the drive. 'Back to Square One', they announced, in a manner that seemed to mock me as I left the Long Room and stepped out into the muggy heat of the last day of July, with the eyes of a 28 000 full house on me.

The gates had been locked soon after the start, which had been very encouraging. But again I was struck by the unshakeable faith of these people, many of whom obviously believed that an overnight miracle had been worked and the series was now ours for the taking.

It seemed very different now, with Lillee breathing fire. All four wickets had fallen to him, three of them l.b.w., and I needed a fair amount of luck to see out his opening spell.

Steele, however, seemed in little trouble. He even had the

audacity to hook Lillee to the boundary on more than one occasion and, together, we restored the balance with a stand of 96 before David left with a half-century to his name.

By the end of the first day we had passed 300 and the 96 I scored were among the sweetest runs of my life. They didn't compare, however, with what happened the next morning as John Snow bowled the old enemy to the brink of surrender.

Something seems to happen to Snowy whenever he comes up against the Australians. He is not quite the same person any more – altogether more mean and hostile. It's small wonder that the Australian players and public have long respected him as one of the finest fast bowlers of recent times – and I suspect they concealed a snigger or two when he wasn't picked to go on the 1974–5 tour of Australia.

Maybe that snub had upset Snow, too, for he seemed intent on reminding everyone at Lord's that his powers were still intact. In his first spell, he fired out Alan Turner and both the Chappell brothers. The crowd were in ecstasies and their roared applause as Snowy returned to fine leg after each over seemed to go on for minutes at a time.

By lunch, they had lost six wickets for about 70 and it all began to seem like a dream. I led the side off, with my heart pumping rowdily, and the reception accorded us in the Long Room was the most emotional thing I ever experienced in an English cricket ground.

The great, cavernous room was packed, and the noise was almost frightening in its intensity. Elderly members, who might normally stir themselves for a ripple of polite clapping, forgot themselves and their condition to jump in the air and cheer. Feet were stamped on the scrubbed and varnished floor, portraits on the wall began to shake and the crazy thought occurred to me that some of the grand old men of cricket portrayed in those paintings might turn in their grave at the unseemly disregard for customary standards.

Every one of us in that team has probably lived that welcome time and again, but it was important at that stage to regain control of emotions and realize that the Australians are never beaten, certainly not at lunchtime on the second day.

And so it proved. Ross Edwards and, remarkably, Dennis Lillee stopped our celebrations and the match was eventually drawn in stalemate.

Leeds was next, with only nine days' break in between. More changes were made and the new cap this time was Phil Edmonds, a slow left-arm bowler from Middlesex. His début was as sensationally successful as that of Steele, who incidentally top scored in both innings here.

Edmonds took five wickets in his first spell and the Aussies were on the run again. We were able to set them 445 in about ten hours. By the close of the fourth day they needed 225 with seven wickets left, but, as both the Chappells were out, I believed we still held a clear advantage.

I was in bed early that night but sleep refused to come. This was the chance I had been awaiting and I was convinced we only needed a reasonable cloud cover the next day for the renowned Headingley swing conditions to help us home.

When morning came at last, I jumped out of bed, threw back the curtains and said my thanks to no one in particular. It was cloudy and, as I went down for breakfast, one–all was almost written on my mind.

It should have been a cheerful, excitable meal, but it wasn't. I had barely started when I was called to the phone. It was Joe Lister, the Yorkshire secretary, in a dreadful state of panic, which was hardly surprising, for what he had to tell me was that the Test pitch had been sabotaged during the night.

Alec Bedser and I drove to the ground in near silence, not daring to consider what we might see. In my mind, I think the awful truth had already been implanted by the description Joe Lister had given me, and I wasn't wrong.

Ian Chappell and I inspected the damage, the holes on a length and the oil splashed randomly, but both of us knew that there was no way of finishing that Test. To stage the last day on a fresh wicket would have been completely wrong – even if we had won, it would not have been the same.

So, instead of taking part in what promised to be a memorable day of cricket, we were driving back down the motorway soon after lunch – ironically through heavy rain which may, in any case, have prevented a positive finish. There might, just might though, have been enough time. . . .

The Oval Test was drawn, although we had been forced to follow on, and the Ashes stayed in Australia. What England badly needed at that point was a winter tour. Not another tour of bouncers and injuries, but a trip on which we could continue the rebuilding operation, increase confidence and mould a squad for the next few years. Instead we had a free winter and our next series was to be a confrontation with the formidable West Indies.

It was neither a lazy nor a wasted winter for me, however. Through contacts I had made on England's tour the previous winter, I was able to accept an invitation to play for the Waverley club in Australia's Sydney premier grade, and combine the cricket with a good deal of work.

Various estimates have been published of how much money I earned during that winter, most of them wildly inaccurate. I must also disillusion the many purveyors of two particular myths : I did not take any money from the Waverley club itself – and I did not make my money by lying on the beach all day and every day.

The business side of the venture was created by a number of men connected with the Waverley club. I was put in touch with various different companies and it was then up to me to negotiate work and terms.

The arrangements worked well. I travelled the country making television commercials for two different companies, I wrote and commentated on the Australia v. West Indies Test series and I worked on a book. It wasn't easy, the hours were long and the work was often tiring. But I enjoyed it all – enjoyed, particularly, learning that if you are prepared to work hard in Australia you will get the financial reward.

I advertised anything from breakfast cereal to underclothes, and the most amusing commercial I undertook involved convincing viewers that a particular brand of ladies' panti-hose called 'Big and Beautiful' could make fat legs look alluringly slim. I still don't know whether anyone believed me !

My family all came out for the winter and we lived in a superb house in Vaucluse, overlooking Sydney harbour and close to where we have since settled. From there, it was no more than a few minutes' walk to the nearest beach, Camp Cove, so I took Samantha and Mark down there on our first day, while Donna sorted the house out.

The first female to walk past was topless and it came as a bit of a shock. On making a few inquiries, however, I found out that Camp Cove was primarily one of Sydney's topless beaches. At first, I didn't let Donna in on my discovery, but, after a few weeks, our English housekeeper joined us and the temptation became too great.

Before going off to work one morning, I suggested that Donna and the housekeeper, who was particularly straight-laced, might like to spend the day at Camp Cove. They agreed it might be a good idea and I left them to it.

I only needed to glance at Donna's expression when I returned late that evening to know that they hadn't missed anything!

The Sydney life-style suited us all and the cricket was just the type I enjoy – a healthy standard and a highly charged atmosphere of competition. The wickets were often a shade rough, which persuaded me to bowl off-breaks, and I fully compensated for not scoring many runs by breaking the grade record for wickets in a season.

Waverley won the premiership for the first time in many years and the enjoyment I gained from the season set me thinking once again that England could benefit from a similar competition.

Anyone who fancies a game of cricket can play – and find his correct level. He could be a dustman or an executive, a Test player or a knock-kneed novice, it wouldn't matter. Waverley alone fielded between six and eight teams every weekend and those who start at the bottom and improve are given every opportunity to move up through the grades.

If you then become good enough to command consideration for a state team, you don't have to give up your regular job because the Sheffield Shield season only involves eight matches each year – and most employers are only too pleased to have a state cricketer working for them.

I did manage to get away from cricket and business for two one-week holidays. For the first, we went up country with some doctors from Sydney with whom we had become friendly, and quickly got involved in the favourite Australian pastime of gambling.

In my experience most Australians will have a bet on anything, and these doctors were no exception. They were keen to play cards, so I taught them a game called three-card brag, commonly played in cricket dressing-rooms around England when rain has stopped play.

It's a simple game, in which you are placing a bet every thirty seconds or so, which appealed to them enormously. The first time we played I took twenty or thirty dollars off them, and I was convinced they had been taking it easy to make sure I played again.

Our next session followed the same pattern – I won again. Soon, I was trying to give some of the money back by playing recklessly. But the bolder I became the more money I won, until eventually I decided it had reached the embarrassing stage and called Donna into the school.

All seemed to be going well, and I noted with a smile of approval that Donna was gaily throwing money in. Naturally, I assumed she was making a pretence of naïvety, but at the end of the hand she turned up three sixes and scooped the pool! I had to give up at that point to save any more red faces.

Later in the season we flew up to the Barrier Reef for a week of fishing and swimming. The fishing there can be quite spectacular, as the difficulty is not so much getting the fish on the hook, but landing them before they are snapped off the line by sharks.

One day, a friend and I had seen some particularly vicious six-foot sharks leaving just the tops of fishes' heads on the hooks, and when we returned to the shore we found Donna and related the story. It transpired that she had been in approximately the same area, constantly falling off water-skis into shark-infested water.

The sharks, for all their faults, do make surprisingly tasty dinners and I ate a proud meal one night after catching a shark and cooking it on the coals with onions and tomatoes.

I returned to England in good health and spirits and found myself named as captain for all five Tests of the coming series against the West Indies. It was a great honour and a great relief, as the axe is lifted slightly from the captain's head with a five-Test appointment. But I had seen enough in Australia to know that we faced a mighty task.

The West Indians had been well beaten by Australia, partly

because their party had lost discipline and fallen into disarray. But the flair and talent were still obvious and they had one young man called Mike Holding who seemed destined for great things.

He is a classically rhythmical West Indian fast bowler and all he had seemed to lack when I saw him against Australia was the right temperament. During the Sydney Test, I was off-duty in the commentary box when Ian Chappell blatantly edged a catch to wicket-keeper Deryck Murray off Holding only to be given 'not out'.

While Holding lay on his back in the middle of the wicket and the West Indians protested volubly to the umpire, Bill Lawry was handing over to Wes Hall in the commentary box, for a talk-through of the action replay.

Hall, a pace-bowling predecessor of Holding with a similarly lithe action, left nobody in any doubts about his feelings. The deflection, he said, was 'unbelievable'. The replay was shown again, and again Hall insisted that the umpire had made a bad mistake.

Holding was still on the grass, sitting with head in hands, and three or four minutes had passed. Lawry now rejoined the commentary with a sideways wink at me, goading Wes with a condemnation of Holding's behaviour.

'This is a disgraceful performance,' said Lawry. 'The umpire has made his decision, and everybody knows that Ian Chappell is not a walker.'

Wes took the bait and turned on him. 'You should know all about that sort of thing,' he retorted. 'I remember getting you caught behind three times in one over and you still wouldn't walk!'

As the rest of us in the box collapsed in helpless laughter, Lance Gibbs finally got the game moving again by picking Holding up and steering him towards the end of his run.

Holding's lack of control was to show itself to me in unpleasant circumstances during the Lord's Test that summer. Enraged by being hit over the top for four, he raced in and unleashed a beamer that I saw only as it hurtled past my nose.

It was an immature and dangerous reaction, whether he intended to bowl it or not. But Holding remains the fastest bowler I have ever faced and, in combination with Wayne Daniel and

Andy Roberts, he provided the West Indies with a pace attack almost to match Lillee and Thomson.

I was chased around the country that summer by the acrimony my 'grovel' remark had stirred up. I have already admitted that it was a mistake, if an unwitting one, but it did not dissuade me from the belief that the game needs people to stand up and be counted every now and then.

By that I don't mean that everyone should adopt slanging tactics and constantly bring the game into disrepute. But it is all too easy to go through life replying to every question with a 'no comment'. England captains of the past have sometimes adopted these tactics and, I believe, done the game no good whatever.

I am, as I've said, something of a press man's dream because, if you talk to me for long enough, I will say something controversial. Occasionally, I am bound to offend someone and get myself into deep water. 'Grovel' was simply an instance of that.

One occasion on which I saved my anger was at Manchester, during the Third Test in 1976. The comments I wanted to make about the wicket for that game might never have appeared in print, but eventually – a whole year later – I did make what I considered to be constructive criticism on the matter. I was promptly disciplined and Sussex were fined for clearing the article, but I will repeat my sentiments here.

We were condemned to face Daniel, Holding and Roberts on what I consider the most dangerous and unpredictable wicket I have ever played a Test match on – and I can never forgive the groundsman or the authorities for allowing it.

On the Saturday evening, two of the bravest English batsmen of my time were reduced to wrecks by a short-pitched assault unparalleled in its danger during my experience. Maybe the bowlers were allowed too many bouncers, but on a respectable wicket the threat would have been halved. How John Edrich and Brian Close survived that session with their wickets and their lives intact I shall never know. Recently to my surprise Brian Close has criticized me for making him open the batting that day. But as far as I was concerned, he and Edrich were by far the best men for the job, so to be honest, Brian's complaint five years later was for me like water off a duck's back and, coming from the tough man that he is, unbelievable.

That Old Trafford Test was the game I shall always remember for all the wrong reasons. It was the first time in my career that I felt really frightened while batting. It was also the first time that I almost gave up.

We were humiliated, bowled out for 71 and 126 and annihilated by more than 400 runs. As I sat in the dressing-room, at the bitter end of it, I felt my whole world had fallen apart. The quick men had finally cast their spell on me and, thanks to that pitch, I had been more concerned with protecting my life than my wicket. I had failed as captain, or so I thought, and I turned to Alan Knott and muttered that I had had enough, that I could handle it no longer.

Knotty told me not to be hasty, led me into a room and talked to me for twenty minutes or so. They were sound words from a sensible fellow and a great friend and he dismissed from my mind any thoughts of resigning.

We went to Headingley 1–0 down, just as we had done against the Australians twelve months previously. This time there was no sabotage and a magnificent match ended in a West Indies win by just 55 runs. It was ironic but satisfying that Knotty and I each scored 116 in our first innings; in the second I was on 76 when I ran out of partners.

The partial revival was purely temporary and we were thrashed again at The Oval. 3–0 to the West Indies constituted a hammering in any language, and the critics were now at my throat.

For the next few weeks I was under real pressure, as conjecture mounted that I might be sacked in favour of Mike Brearley for the coming tour of India. Brearley, however, was not at that stage an established member of the England side and I accept that it was probably that fact as much as anything else that persuaded the selectors to reappoint me. They no doubt also acknowledged that I could scarcely have wished for eight tougher Tests with which to start and that the resources at my command had not exactly been mighty.

Brearley was elected vice-captain for a tour that was to herald the start of England's revival and paint the outline of a team to regain the Ashes in 1977.

One of the best shots I played towards the winning of that series was made before we had set foot on a cricket ground. During the

E

press conference which a captain traditionally faces at the start of a tour, I was asked for my views on Indian umpires.

The question was expected, because New Zealand's captain Glenn Turner had left India in a blaze of anger directed at the country's umpiring standards, only a fortnight before our arrival.

My answer had been ready for some time, and I told the Indian journalists that their country possessed some of the best umpires in the world. I was not prepared to venture any criticism until they had been given a fair chance – and I made it quite clear that there was to be no dissent from the England players.

It was a diplomatic stroke of which I am proud, for we only suffered from controversial decisions in one Test – and by that time the series was already won.

John Lever gave us the ideal start by taking ten wickets on his début as we won the First Test at Delhi early on the fifth day. It was my first win as captain and gave me a marvellous feeling. But we had won at Delhi four years earlier, only to lose the series. I didn't intend to let that happen again.

I 2

A week in the life

Six o'clock on Christmas night. Traditionally, perhaps the most peaceful and relaxed time in any year. But in Calcutta in 1976 it was the moment which Greig selected to deliver a singularly unfestive surprise to his MCC team.

A seasonal spirit of bonhomie prevailed in the team room on the second floor of the city's Grand Hotel, as the players gathered for what they supposed to be a Christmas night drink with the management. And why not? The Delhi Test had been convincingly won, the team were heroes in Calcutta and most had enjoyed a Christmas Day of food and drink, uncluttered with cricket concerns. Was it not natural that they should now meet for a sociable evening?

Some were late in arriving. One, unaware that this was anything more significant than a beer with the boys, allowed himself to be detained elsewhere and failed to appear. But inside the room, an indication of what was to come saw manager Ken Barrington dismiss, politely but firmly, the journalists who had been invited in for a drink by the players.

When all was calm Greig stood up and swore violently. For more than twenty minutes he raged at the players, collectively and individually, castigating them for slack discipline and reminding them, with a number of irreverent words, of their purpose in India.

It was neither an orthodox team-talk nor a particularly fitting outburst for Christmas night. But it was to have its desired effect in days to come, as Greig moved into the week he considers the most rewarding of his spell as England's captain. The events and emotions of these seven days in Calcutta were recorded in diary form, and are reproduced here.

Day One: New Year's Eve 1976

Relief and anticipation are fighting for prominence in my mind tonight. The relief is provided by the justification of my shock tactics on Christmas night; the anticipation by the imminence of the crunch. The Calcutta Test begins tomorrow morning; the team is picked, our final net preparations are complete, the pre-Test dinner is over. Tonight is New Year's Eve, but no time for revels. Tomorrow is far too important.

We are now approaching this match in exactly the right mood of determination, yet a week ago my concern over team discipline was growing uncomfortably – hence the Christmas night 'scene'.

Our win in Delhi had only reminded me of the 1972–3 tour and filled me with the obsession to ensure that we did not continue the pattern, lose our lead in Calcutta and lose the series in Madras.

A combination of the First Test victory and the time of year had induced a noticeable relaxation among the players. It was dangerous and had to be curbed, but I was equally conscious that team spirit could only be harmed by curtailing or cancelling the players' right to celebrate Christmas. So I waited.

On Christmas Eve, Keith Fletcher flaked an ankle bone in a fall during a party. He was helped back to the hotel and it wasn't until the next morning that a hospital examination revealed the damage. So we stood to lose a critical member of the team – and it angered me. The accident was nobody's fault, but it had illogically triggered my fear to a point at which something had to be done.

I allowed the day to pass in the traditional manner, myself enjoying turkey and Christmas pudding at the home of one of Calcutta's British High Commission officials. By late afternoon I was back at the hotel, spreading the word about our team meeting at six.

We were due to fly out of Calcutta early the next morning and, apart from the knowledge that we were heading for a town called Gauhati on the lower Himalayan slopes, our destination could have been classified unknown. MCC officials had searched maps in vain for a mention of the place, while local reports only advised us that it was an area to be avoided by choice. But we had no choice; it was to be our only game before Calcutta, conditions seemed likely to be unpleasant and I believed our players were in no mental state to tackle it.

Something was necessary to jolt them back into an awareness of priorities, and I elected for a verbal assault.

When I am angry, my language can deteriorate. That night it was appalling and, as I ranted through my criticisms, my gaze swept the stunned room, finally resting on Alan Knott. There is little on a cricket tour that can surprise Knotty any more, but his eyes were wide and startled. The message, though not directed at him, was clearly being appreciated.

I didn't wait for answers, nor did I hang around to share a drink with anyone. That would have been incongruous. Instead, having got everything off my chest, I strode out, slamming the door on an extraordinary silence.

It wasn't long afterwards that Ken Barrington, our manager, returned to his living room and found me there with a cup of coffee, a quizzical smile on my face. 'I have heard some strong talks before,' he said. 'But that one beat the lot.'

Naturally, I ran the risk of inciting an element of resentment. But I had enough faith in the dedication of these players to discount that possibility. The last few days have proved me right, too.

Gauhati was anything but the hell-hole it had been painted. We were treated royally in breathtaking surroundings and the game acted as an ideal warm-up, a chance for everyone to shake off the excesses of weight and lethargy left over from Christmas.

Three of the seniors – Knott, Amiss and Fletcher – had stayed behind for a three-day break in Calcutta. Ideally, we wanted all three in the Test team, but when we returned here yesterday, Fletcher's ankle was no better. He needed assistance even to walk, and there could be no question of him playing.

Now we have another worry. Derek Underwood is the latest victim of the stomach complaint that is as much a part of India as the common cold is of England. The possibility that he might not make it in time is an undesirable one, especially considering the reputation of the Calcutta wicket as a spinners' heaven.

Most of the younger players had their first view of the Eden Gardens ground when we reported there for net practice yesterday afternoon. For me, though, it was a nostalgic trip. New stands have been built since I was here four years ago, but the popular terraces are the same – great steepling blocks of wooden benches towering up into the sky, topped by the largest advertisement hoarding I have ever seen. I stood in the middle, the stadium empty apart from our squad, and imagined how it will be tomorrow – a colourful, emotional bowl where it is sometimes impossible to think above the howling din of 80 000 Indians.

The bus transported us back to the hotel without Derek Randall. He stayed behind, batting intently in the nets and scorning all those who still look upon him as a clown in flannels. Sure, he's a comic, but under the exterior lies a fierce pride in his own performance and that of the team. Whether or not he meant to miss the bus I don't know, but he certainly had no intention of leaving until he was happy with his form.

At lunchtime today Derek was duly named to replace Fletcher in the Test side. It is to be his first cap, but it was by no means the most difficult decision we had to make. That, without question, was the dropping of Bob Woolmer in favour of Roger Tolchard.

I had been strongly behind the choice of Tolchard for this tour and I've taken some stick for it. He had come, superficially, as reserve wicket-keeper, although I admit he is nothing like the second best in England. I wanted him for his qualities as a batsman against the spinners, a guarantee against the injuries we are now beginning to suffer.

Woolmer, however, has been out of form, unable to adapt to the demands of turning wickets after two summers against pace. Our selectors were split on it, but Tolchard won the vote. It was then down to me to break the news to Bob, and I took him aside in the corridor before we announced the side to the players. The consoling arm around the shoulder and the encouraging words that every place is still open can never really compensate for a cap, and I was uncomfortably conscious that this was one of the captaincy duties I was not keen on.

I slept this afternoon, waking in time for the customary eve-of-

Test dinner, but my sleep was seldom untroubled. I now know just how important the toss will be tomorrow, and it worries me.

It had always seemed likely that a spinners' wicket would be produced here in an attempt to favour India's battery of slow bowlers. But the extraordinary spectacle I witnessed on the ground this morning exceeded my wildest imagination.

The pitch looked reasonable when we arrived for our final net session; hardly grassy, but with enough of a covering to suggest that batting might not be too hazardous for at least the first couple of days. Then, as I watched, half a dozen of the ground-staff labourers trooped out to the wicket armed with wire scrubbing brushes and proceeded to use them on the Test pitch.

As they dragged the brushes up and down the pitch in teams of two, removing every blade of living grass, I confronted the groundsman and demanded to know what they were up to. His answer led me nowhere; it was 'normal practice'. There was no way I could officially intervene with the preparation of the wicket, so I elected to make my feelings known in a silent fashion; I returned to the dressing-room and collected my camera.

Eventually, after I had circled the labourers, snapping the treatment and the effect from every angle, an Indian official emerged to call them off. It was too late to save the pitch and, for all I know, they may even have returned later. But at least I had made my point.

The obvious effect of this crude scrubbing will be to transform the wicket into a raging turner – and it wouldn't surprise me if it turned from the first morning. Heaven help the team which has to bat last on that . . . and we may not even have Derek Underwood to exploit it.

Day Two: New Year's Day 1977

You can, at least, wake up cool in this hotel, thanks to the wonders of air conditioning. In Calcutta you can never be cool for long. A five-minute street walk can leave you sweating; walk the short distance across the rambling park from hotel to cricket ground and you become a damp, dirty mess. Fires burn on the parkland, or *Maidan*, fumes belch at you from the crazy, incessant traffic as you cross the roads, pungent smells from the refuse assault your senses as you tramp across the rough grass.

That walk was not for us this morning, but thousands of others were making it. I could see them from the hotel windows as I went down to breakfast; swarms of excited ants heading in a single direction, the precious match tickets clutched in their sticky palms. It was a sight that churned my stomach, adding to the already acute sensation that I was about to be part of something special.

Breakfast-time brought the good news – Derek Underwood declared himself fit enough to play. I knew in my heart that he was anything but 100 per cent, but a spot of cruel psychology had worked in my favour.

'Deadly', you see, missed the vital Third Test on our previous Indian tour, four years ago, because he lay out in the sun for far too long and subsequently suffered sunstroke. I had often teased him about that since, for the Test had been lost and I knew he blamed himself. These past few days, I have constantly reminded him, imposed on his conscience as it were. Call it unfair if you will, but he opted to play because he felt he had to – and that was the object.

The morning meal was as edgy as it always is before a Test. Nerve ends exposed themselves here and there, especially in Derek Randall, who was reduced to a bundle of nervous energy. Some find it hard to eat before a Test, but I went through my regular routine and consumed a hearty breakfast. Bob Willis and I ate our normal pre-match energy product, mixed in porridge.

Breakfast here is eaten in a coffee shop situated on the pool-side. From there to the hotel foyer is a walk of maybe thirty yards down a corridor. All the way back the noise level rose and, as I emerged in the foyer, I was amazed to see it overrun with people – some match officials, most just hangers-on. All of them were staring at us.

If that was unnerving for our 'rookies', it was nothing compared to the reception in the street. Police cordons linked arms to hold back the thousands massed outside the hotel and the team bus could only be reached by running the gauntlet across the pavement as the crowds surged forward.

Once aboard, the problems are still not over. The ground, as

I've said, is a short walk across the park, but by road it seemed to take an eternity. Indian drivers are neither the best nor the most courteous in the world and, on this particular morning, the whole country seemed to be heading for Eden Gardens. The route was an unbroken mass of metal, horns blaring in an incessant, illogical concerto. As the stadium loomed, the going just got slower.

Finally we were there, nosing through the throng of excited faces on the gate and reaching the unreal calm of the dressing-room. Some of the boys could bottle it all up no longer. They dropped their bags and burst out on to the pitch to begin their exercise routine. Others, myself included, took things more sedately. I enjoyed a cigarette and a cup of tea, alone with my thoughts in a corner of the room.

I went outside eventually and it was just as I remembered it : full, frenetic, uplifting. Our boys were going through their well-practised schedule, the fast bowlers supervised by physio Bernard Thomas, a few others jogging and Alan Knott noticeably alone, stretching, bending and accepting imaginary catches – the warm-up pattern of a remarkable, priceless player.

The toss was the big event I had expected. The crowd were knowledgeable enough to realize the importance of it and their emotions were near boiling point as I walked out with Bishen Bedi, resplendent in his blue patka. It was odd to think that the match could effectively be over once we had spun this lump of metal; I was convinced it was essential to call correctly. I didn't though, it fell for India and Bedi leaped high, arms thrown in the air, as if he too considered the game in their pocket. The noise of the crowd exploded in my ears, and the walk back was a lonely, slightly despondent one. None of the players had to be told we were in the field; the scene had said it all.

Many of them needed cajoling, picking up, and the need for a brave face from me was paramount. A quick chat and we were out, the crowd rising to us generously with that multi-coloured patchwork effect that characterizes Indian crowds. There was not a space to be seen anywhere and they all wanted to be enter-tained. Derek Randall, I believed, could help.

Derek had already claimed a reputation on the tour for clown-ing. His cartwheels had become famous, his dance with the umpire was a party piece. But here he was, making his Test début and, naturally, apprehensive of overplaying the comic act. I did my best to reassure him, told him to act the fool as he pleased because the crowd would love him for it. They did, too. He was off before the first ball had been delivered, flicking his sun-hat in the air and catching it on his head. Periodically, throughout the scorching day, he repeated his hat-trick, somersaulted, or slouched into an outrageous, swaggering walk. It all set him up as an idol for the rest of the series.

By the time the first over was complete, any complacency India may have felt must have disappeared. Sunil Gavaskar, fortunate not to touch Bob Willis's fizzing opening ball, was not so lucky with the third and Chris Old took a superb one-handed catch to his left at third slip. 'Sunny' was the man we wanted; his wicket, so early, was a psychological triumph.

One man on our side hadn't seen the start of the over, however. Down at fine leg, Derek Underwood was feeling wretched and, as Willis raced in to begin the Test, Derek had lurched away and vomited. It left no further room for doubt that he had been brave even to play. Now he was braver still to see it out and field for almost six hours in blazing heat.

The Indians didn't put up much resistance today. We have always suspected that their batting is weak and, here again, our seamers found them out. Willis took three wickets in the day, John Lever two and Chris Old one. They finished at 146 for seven, but it was no time to pat ourselves on the back and relax. To win, we simply had to get them out cheaply twice and avoid any sort of fourth-innings target.

Escaping from the ground is as difficult as reaching it, and for a while there was no point in trying. Even after a half-hour rest in the dressing-room, the bus still had to disperse a sizeable crowd. As we roared past, one or two of the bolder fans tried to hang on to the bus, only to be thrown aside by the speed. Fanatics, all of them.

The team-room was our base for the whole evening. We insist that everyone pops in each night, if only for a swift drink. But tonight no one wanted to leave and we talked for more than two hours. I've rarely known a team so intent on winning a game.

Day Three: 2 January

I woke with that familiar sense of impatience gnawing at me. Breakfast was a bore, the drive to the ground dragged. I couldn't wait to get at them again and finish the job, yet, at the back of my mind, a niggling doubt about our own batting potential kept making itself known. I fought it.

Last night's togetherness had left everyone bubbling and we came on to the field soccer-style. I was scarcely out of the gate at the head of the team before Randall sprinted past, then Barlow, Willis and Tolchard. It was an exuberant entrance that set off a murmur of expectancy in another vast crowd on another inevitably sunny morning.

Willis bowled like a man possessed and finished them off clinically. They are scared of him, there can be no doubt of that. In appearance he is so different from the Indians – huge in height, fierce in expression, Afro hair bouncing round his sharp-featured face. What's more, he is fast. This wicket has nothing for him, but I've never seen him bowl quicker.

Bob has had so many problems in the past that this is like starting again. He has had to make a huge effort to regain fitness and, every morning, he completes a series of exercises in the dressing-room. Surprisingly, for one of his humour and character, nerves are a big part of his make-up. He sleeps badly and has suffered more than most out here. Today he made it though, and I was delighted for him.

The worst was to come; we all knew that. Getting them out for 155 was one thing. Making that many ourselves against all the odds was something else. Graham Barlow was down to open, for the first time in a Test, and I could tell him nothing more profound than to be natural. I did make it very plain to each of the batsmen, however, that if they got in I expected no reckless shots. Once settled, they must stay there.

Our early batting had shuddered during the win in Delhi and it was the part of our armoury that caused me most of my worries. Today I prayed for a change, but, at least at first, nobody heard me.

The seamers, such as they are, bowled only three overs between them – enough, though, for Madan Lal to dismiss poor Barlow.

A tumultuous roar then announced that Bedi had decided to take things in hand. As the ground sang in excitement, our dressing-room was a solitary frozen patch in the cauldron. A glance around the faces told the story. No one was arrogant now, the confidence had drained. One or two of the comics, Randall and Lever I think, tried a joke, but it was too strained to work. Amazing really, that we should all seize up because one man is about to bowl. It is a complex we must get rid of.

As Bedi jogged those few strides to the wicket the din increased – rather as soccer crowds in England roar a goal-keeper through his run-up for a goal-kick. They expected some sort of magic, and I suppose they got it. Brearley didn't last the over. He played a wooden shot, as if overcome by the atmosphere, and short leg held a simple catch.

Randall lapped delightfully for 37, then departed, and Dennis Amiss followed. The spinners, the weavers of India's magic, had broken us down again and the masses were screaming for blood as I went out at 90 for four. I was nervous, as I always am before a Test innings. I swung my arms in the windmill action that began as a loosening exercise but has become a trademark. I expect I looked calm enough, but I was aware that this was to be one of my most important knocks for my country.

It was around tea-time when I got to the wicket, devoid of any thoughts of heroics. The priority was simply to be there tomorrow morning and my head went down accordingly. Roger Tolchard was at the other end and coping very nicely with a brand of dancing footwork against the spinners. I preferred to play them from the crease and the combination at least gave them something extra to think about.

Prasanna, the master off-spinner, scarcely dropped a ball off line and, as the close field crept nearer still, I decided to gamble. The next ball that he pitched up slightly too far disappeared over mid wicket for six. I was proud of the shot and it had been a calculated risk. Sure enough, the field dispersed enough to give me breathing space. The close arrived. Tolchard is still with me.

The last session was gruelling. Every ball demanded maximum concentration and I felt drained as I climbed the stairs to the dressing-room. Willis was waiting at the door and he greeted me with an action that said more than any words could have done. Reaching out as I passed, he grabbed my sweat-sodden arm and squeezed the shirt-sleeve. This was the bowler who had set it all up for us and watched us come so close to throwing it all away. Bob lives every ball of a Test; he has a compulsion to watch, yet he punishes himself by doing so. I knew his gesture was one of appreciation, coupled with the urge to keep going.

Tonight I've had time to reflect on the strange lot of the captain. Last night we were well placed and I needed to keep everyone's feet on the ground. Now we are struggling, everything we feared has happened, and it was my duty to drag them all up, tell them it was all still possible.

I've got a problem of my own, too. Maybe the sun got through to me more than I thought, but I got back to the hotel feeling pretty unwell. I couldn't force any food down and I've felt a bit sick all evening. Bernie Thomas has given me some sleeping pills and I'm turning in early.

Day Four: 3 January

One of the longest, most uncomfortable and most fulfilling days of my life. I began it soon after midnight this morning with a high fever, completed it this evening with 94 not out and victory a clear possibility.

My bedclothes were saturated when I emerged from a restless sleep in the early hours. Yet my teeth were chattering and my entire body was shaking with them. I got into a hot bath to warm me up, then asked the bearer to change the bedclothes and tried to sleep again. It was hopeless. First the sweats, then the shivers – classic evidence of fever. I gave up, reached out a tired arm to the phone and asked to be put through to Bernard Thomas.

It was three in the morning when I woke Bernie, but he showed neither surprise nor annoyance – the complete professional, as ever. There was, of course, little he could do. A few tablets were distributed from his medicine case, then he simply told me to try and sleep and forget about the time. He would wake me, he said.

Sleep didn't come easily and I spent the last five hours of the night tossing and turning, the discomfort of my condition mixing with the despair that I should be ill on this of all nights.

I never once considered the unthinkable – that I should be too ill to continue my innings. It didn't matter how sick I might be, I knew I had to be there. The only way I could have stayed in bed would have been if Bernard had told me I would kill myself by getting out. But, when he woke me from a fitful doze at eight o'clock, the only information he passed was that my temperature was 104; about the number of runs I needed to score.

As a rule, I look forward to breakfast and enjoy it. Today it was a necessary evil. I wanted to force some food down and, thankfully, I managed to keep it down. I didn't enter into much conversation, either during the meal or on the way to the ground – my energy needed conserving.

Once inside the stadium, I planted myself on my dressing-room seat and stayed there until the last possible moment, drinking as much as possible under Bernie's direction. It is at times like this that the real value of a man like Bernie becomes apparent. Not only is he a fine physio and a very knowledgeable medical man, but he also possesses the priceless gift of man-management; he understands us all and treats us accordingly. He knew exactly how I needed nursing this morning and, apart from administering the odd tablet and drink, he left me alone – just as I would have wished him to.

I think the crowd brought me round as much as anything. They seem to have remembered me from the last trip, when I tried the clowning bit on them and, as Roger Tolchard and I walked out on to the ground this morning, they rose quite unexpectedly, cheering us to the wicket as if we were on their side. I would be a liar if I said I didn't enjoy the adulation of crowds, and today it was a comforting noise.

My fear, I suppose, was that the sun would only aggravate the fever and make it progressively more difficult for me to go on. But, instead, the occasion, the state of the game and the application it demanded, overpowered every other feeling in my body and I was able to forget how ill I was supposed to be.

Two other factors inspired me. The first was the batting of Tolchard and, as he moved on towards fifty, I felt a sense of pride for him. He justified all my hopes and statements with his handling of the spinners, which at times was outrageously bold. Prasanna was the danger, but 'Tolly' rarely allowed him to bounce. He didn't shuffle or walk down the pitch, he ran to meet the ball as it dropped – a frustration to any spinner.

His runs came chiefly from dabs and glances and every one was vital. When he had made 59 Prasanna outsmarted him, firing the ball wide down the leg side as Roger advanced. He was stumped by feet, but his part had been played.

The second inspiration was the continuous presence of Ken Barrington. He could scarcely have got himself nearer to the action as he sat on the boundary, next to the sightscreen, and studied intently. Every time I turned he was there – in fact, he never moved from his seat throughout the day, perhaps through a suspicion that I would get out if he did.

I have often talked at length with Ken about the various techniques of playing spin on a turner and it was probably fascination at my methods as much as anything else which riveted him to his seat.

Against the off-spinners I played in orthodox fashion, but I countered Bedi by taking off-stump guard, then standing outside it and kicking away a good proportion of his efforts.

It was a technique I had learned many years ago after reading a book by the South African Hughie Tayfield in which he selected Harry Birrell as the most effective player of spin bowling he had encountered. Birrell, at the time, was manager of the South African Schools side, and when I met him I asked him to explain his theories.

He said that most batsmen take a normal guard and fail to protect themselves against the deliveries most likely to get them out. A slow left-armer, for instance, is looking to find the edged catch to slip or gully, or to overstretch the batter outside off stump and have him stumped. It is essential, he went on, to take up the best position from which you can play the ball on the face of the bat and, against this sort of bowling, a leg-stump guard is useless. His advice was to get as far to the off as is comfortable, and I took his theory to its limit today.

I made no attempt to push the score along, because it would have been suicidal. I found that out early on, when Chandrasekhar threw up a ball of full length and I went to drive. It lobbed in the air and dropped invitingly in the unoccupied mid-off position, running for four but convincing me that the drive was just not on.

The rest of my runs came from cuts and pulls – and they came slowly. This was only the third day, but the ball was turning and lurching, making batting difficult enough and quick scoring unthinkable. For much of the day I forced myself on with the thought that the next Test is at Madras, the Indians' most successful ground. Whatever happens, we must not lose here; and I considered it crucial that I stayed until tomorrow.

I don't remember ever batting through an entire day before and to those back in England who know my style it must be a mystery how I contrived to add no more than 70 today. But we are in front now and every run we add is another they need to score to make us bat again.

At the end of it Willis was at the door again, just as he'd been at the start of each interval through the day. He looked as exhausted as I felt.

Day Five: 4 January

Last evening passed almost as a void. I was shattered, I know that much, and it was simply a question of eating a plain meal – nothing that might excite the fever again – and getting back to bed.

A sound sleep made all the difference. I was still tired when I woke this morning, but my temperature was back to normal and I was comforted by the thought that this was our rest day. Tests in India generally begin on Saturdays, continuing on Sunday and Monday with Tuesday as the day off.

Some players like to make the most of the rest day by playing golf, going to the beach – if you happen to be near enough – or shopping for presents. But my routine is generally a relaxing one : a late breakfast in the restaurant – I detest having breakfast in bed – a morning spent lazing around the swimming pool, a light lunch and an afternoon sleep, followed by dinner fairly late and bed just before midnight.

Today was necessarily different, as I had little intention of moving very far from my bed. Bernie advises me that rest is now the best method of dispersing the after-effects and, with a century dangling like a carrot, I need to feel refreshed tomorrow.

The first part of the day was taken up by a press conference at 10 a.m. An unusual one, really, as I conducted it from my bed like a wounded hero. The journalists tend to grow into the team party on any tour, becoming just like another part of the family, and this morning they were beaming patriotically.

After the obvious inquiries about my condition, the questions began to fire in concerning the state of the wicket. Beyond some vague reference to it being a pity that a Test in such a marvellous stadium should be so affected by pitch conditions, I refused to be drawn, seeing no sense in upsetting everybody just when things were beginning to work out for us. If they want to write about the scrubbing-brush preparation, let them make their own comments.

When they had departed to their rooms and typewriters, I lay in a quiet pool of satisfaction and felt well enough to think about getting up. As always, bearers (room servants) were on tap – they would change the bed every ten minutes if I wanted them to. Each time one appeared with, say, a pot of coffee, he would cast his eyes around the room until they alighted on something out of place, like a stray sock lying on the floor. He would then replace it in the correct drawer, tidying clothes as he did so, and feel cheated if he was asked to leave before everything was back in apple-pie order. The exit would then be made backwards, bowing at every step.

To them it is an honour to be able to serve. There is never a hint of complaint and they will do absolutely anything they are asked. I hear so much nonsense talked about the standard of service and hygiene in Indian hotels; I wish the perpetrators would go out and see it as it really is.

I did get up for a while later today, but accomplished nothing more energetic than a walk out to the swimming pool. The streets of Calcutta are uninviting at any time and today they were repellent. My face is now so known here that I would not have been able to set foot outside the door without being pawed by beggars, autograph hunters and maybe even the odd common thief. For all its raw excitement, Calcutta is still a noisy, smelly, overcrowded place and I was certainly not up to facing it today.

This evening I ate early and went to bed feeling just about ready to resume the fight tomorrow. I had to hide a smile as I entered my room, past the stocky guard with rifle on shoulder. There would be no interruptions tonight.

Day Six: 5 January

We nearly made it in four days. India have hung on thanks to an unbroken eighth-wicket stand of 48 between Patel and Prasanna, but they still need 21 even to make us bat again. The odds are now so heavily in our favour that it is difficult not to adopt a celebratory mood prematurely.

I felt well again this morning and the century duly arrived – occupying, I'm told, all of seven hours. Prasanna dismissed me l.b.w. for 103, but Chris Old went on to score a half-century that was incongruously aggressive and we were finally all out with a lead of 166. I thought we might still need every one.

India got to lunch with the openers still together, but they shouldn't have done. Just before the break I came on to bowl myself, and Gavaskar obligingly miscued straight to mid off. I was in the process of acclaiming the breakthrough when Dennis Amiss spilled the dolly. Dennis felt sick and at the time it assumed a significance that was later disproved.

Neither Gavaskar nor Gaekwad lasted long into the afternoon and, when little 'Vishy' Viswanath lazily clipped me to John Lever at mid wicket, India were 30-odd for three and I thought they were beginning to despair. Vishy can be one of the world's finest players when he's going well, but today he looked like a man who had given it all up.

The wicket was still turning and Underwood was wheeling maiden after maiden. But Sharma and Patel played him safely for a long period and I was left with a decision to make. I decided on Bob Willis, who had been skulking around with the air of someone unfairly out of a job.

Bob tends to vary his run nowadays, but this afternoon he went back almost to the sightscreen. It seemed a perverse action, considering the intense heat out there, but Bob later explained that it gave him a longer break between each ball. I wasn't going to argue.

Two catches by Knotty got rid of Sharma and Solkar, both Willis victims, and we were back on the road. Now, for the first time, the crowd began to turn. Until now they had remained good-humoured even with their side in trouble, but the demise of Solkar incited their stronger passions.

In 1972 Ekkie Solkar had been a god to them. He was a superb close catcher and no mean bat and I remember the acclaim he received during our tour under Tony Lewis – especially for one diving catch off a bottom-edged pull from Lewis himself that was so brave it was almost foolish. That had been at Calcutta, where the crowd had adored him. Now he was their villain and, as he retreated morosely to the pavilion, oranges and paper cups rained down on his head.

I felt sorry for Ekkie, who had once been a team-mate of mine at Sussex, but I also felt concerned at the changing heart of this vast audience. It is hard to forget that Calcutta is renowned for riots and, as the Indian team sank lower, so the disturbances along the back of the terracing grew more frequent. They were nothing serious, a couple of minor scuffles really, but I thought the time had come to humour them.

For the next hour or so Randall and I tried every trick we knew. I would go down on my knees in prayer to them, then Derek would throw his hat in the air. I would pretend to shoot them all, then Derek would shake his fist and fall flat on his face. People may think that these sort of actions have no place on an international cricket pitch, but the desired effect was achieved and any potential disorder was quelled.

Patel cheered them anyway and, when Prasanna joined him at 95 for seven, he opened out into a display of attacking shots that seemed quite unfitting in the circumstances. The Indians have often said that Patel is only at his best when the game is beyond saving. Today, I hope, he was too late again, but we have reached the stage where this partnership must be broken.

In the team-room this evening I've been trying to keep everyone calm – yes, the wheel has turned again – and stressing that India only need to get 100 ahead, admittedly unlikely, to cause us real aggravation. Against that sort of fourth-innings target the early loss of a few wickets could mean disaster, and I hate to contemplate losing from this position.

Day Seven: 6 January

Our first and only mistake of an unforgettable day was to under-estimate the Indian cricket supporter. With the possibility that the match could have been over in less than half an hour, we anticipated a small crowd and left our departure much later than normal. How wrong can you be?

The bus spent an age trying to negotiate the route; the traffic, if anything, was worse than on any previous morning. The impossible supposition was confirmed when we raced into the ground only a few minutes before the scheduled start and looked out on 80 000 fans, the fifth full house of the match. I don't believe that would have happened anywhere else in the world.

At least our miscalculations meant that there was no hanging around to be done, no chance for the butterflies to start biting. We were into the action quickly, applauding Patel's half-century, worrying over an extravagant burst of hitting from Bedi that couldn't last – or could it? We bowled them out for 181, Underwood finishing with three wickets when he might have had seven with a slice of luck.

It was reality at last. With only 16 wanted, we could not fail now. Graham Barlow was almost out once or twice, but we got there with all ten wickets intact and I've rarely seen a more exuberant dressing-room.

The television cameras wanted me, radio interviewers wanted me, the press wanted me. But, for the moment, all I could think about was the team and the result – and that wonderful, crazy crowd.

Despite the worries of the previous afternoon, they took defeat warm-heartedly. In fact, they had been so grateful to see as much play as they did on the final day that the run with which India saved an innings defeat was greeted with a roar that would have done justice to a victory.

Now, they clearly didn't want to go home. The noise was filtering through to the dressing-room, where a couple of bottles of champagne were already being popped, and I decided to take the team out to them again. It turned into a triumphant, frantic lap of honour, and they cheered us every step of the way.

Armed police ran around with us, but they weren't needed.

There was no hint of violence, although my tour blazer was torn somehow on the way, and as soon as we disappeared into the pavilion again, the crowd began to disperse, satisfied with a morning's entertainment for a full day's money.

In the interviews that followed I talked genuinely about the most emotional day I've had as England's captain, and about the spirit that has run through this team, embracing even those who are not in the side. They have all been marvellous, nursing the players through with food, drink and especially encouragement. It all seemed a long way from my Christmas night explosion, but I still don't regret it.

Back at the hotel the celebrations began in earnest in early afternoon. But for me, champagne always comes as something of an anti-climax after the real excitement of the triumph. I don't even like it much – so I drank tea instead.

13

Goodbye to all that?

India had been conquered, despite a scandalous character assault on John Lever in Madras and almost laughable umpiring standards in Bangalore. The series ended 3–1 in England's favour and was a greater triumph than those at home can possibly have appreciated. The hazards of Indian cricket can only be measured by personal experience, but suffice it to say that playing the Indians on their own soil is a very different proposition from meeting them in England.

Sri Lanka, the intermediate, flag-waving stopover, was completed uncomfortably, the withering humidity hardly endearing itself to anyone. Still to come was what many considered the highspot of the tour – a fortnight in Australia, climaxing in the Centenary Test Match. As a game, it captured the attention of the cricket world; thousands in England stayed up all night to listen to live commentary of the gripping last day. But, although precious few people realized it at the time, the Centenary Test also formed the backdrop for the organization of the most devastating coup cricket has ever known . . . the Kerry Packer take-over.

The real delight of the Indian tour was in the opportunity to test one's batting talents against the subtle skills of world-class bowlers . . . with no risk of injury. It had been a long battle against the world's most accomplished spinners, yet an enlightening and facinating one. After three consecutive series against the most hostile pace bowlers in cricket, the spinners provided a different game – just as difficult, but with the fear element removed.

Not everyone, however, had been able to cut himself off completely from the torture he had suffered against the likes of Lillee. Dennis Amiss, for one, talked frequently of his problems against pace and it was clear to me that, for him, the real fight of the trip was to come at the end, in Melbourne.

Perth was first, however, and we reached it at an unearthly hour. It was around six in the morning when we landed – a bright, crisp morning on which it would generally have been a joy to be alive. But we had been travelling for eighteen hours since leaving Colombo's stifling shores, four of them spent sitting and strolling aimlessly at Singapore airport.

Sleep was the first essential and we grabbed at it. But, all too soon, it was afternoon, the only time available to us for a net session. The very next day we were due to begin the final leg of the tour with a three-day game against Western Australia, champions of the Sheffield Shield.

I glanced at the papers when I got up and didn't need to look far for the big cricket story; Dennis Lillee had said he was unlikely to be available for the coming tour of England. His reasons were unclear, although I was later to appreciate them in detail. For the moment I was far more concerned with the supplementary announcement that Lillee would, however, be playing in both the Western Australia game and the Centenary Test.

At the WACA ground that afternoon I was met by Barry Richards, who had been spending the English off-season playing and coaching in Perth. Like Lillee, Richards had a secret to keep – and he kept it.

We drew in Perth, with the only damage being to Amiss's pride as Lillee resumed his haunting. The flight across country to Melbourne takes four hours and we arrived to the expected press gathering and an unexpected escort to our hotel – a helicopter which hovered over the coach all along the route.

The Hilton, our base for ten days of history, was cluttered with faces and voices from cricket's past. Larwood, Hutton, Compton and Edrich, Lindwall and Miller, Johnston, Hassett – they were all here and, if you allowed yourself to be affected by it, you would soon be overpowered.

Somehow we had to cut ourselves off, play our game, yet, at the same time, not be disrespectful to our predecessors during an occasion that belonged as much to them as it did to us.

Gala matches like this, however serious their intent, so often fall flat that there was almost an anticipation of anti-climax. But it never happened. We bowled them out cheaply, they dismissed us in turn for next to nothing, then the Test changed face. A century from Rod Marsh helped Australia set us an almost inconceivable 463 for victory – yet we came so close that half of England apparently discarded a night's sleep in favour of the radio broadcast of the final day's play.

Derek Randall scored a century that was priceless for our chances, his personal future – and the stature of the side. It had been all too easy for those at home to remark glibly that 'any team could have beaten India', which was neither accurate nor reasonable. Randall's ton brought us agonizingly close to a win that would have proved so much more.

While all but a handful of our squad headed for home the morning after the climax, I stayed behind to look up a few business contacts and keep an appointment with a man I was very keen to meet. His name was Kerry Packer.

At this point it is necessary for me to make one thing very clear. *I* had made the appointment with Mr Packer and I had made it purely to sound him out on the possibility of earning some money by broadcasting on his television network. I was already making plans for the following winter and I hoped to fill the two months between the end of our season and England's departure for Pakistan with some lucrative work in Australia. Television commentating was something that appealed to me and Packer was one of the big names in the business.

I arrived at his home in Bellevue Hill, Sydney, without the slightest knowledge of the plan he had already set in motion which was destined to shake the cricket establishments of the world. Many people have since been openly sceptical when I have made this assertion, but I make it again now, while accepting how odd it must seem to the uninvolved. For the Packer plan was the best-kept secret I have ever been part of.

Barry Richards and Dennis Lillee had been among the first to sign for him. I know them both well, and spent a fair amount of time with each of them in Perth – yet neither breathed a word about the scheme.

In Melbourne, I learned later, the best illustration of the secrecy was provided by a dialogue between Greg Chappell and Rod Marsh, respectively captain and vice-captain of the Australian team. Chappell had accepted a Packer contract during Australia's short tour of New Zealand in February, but Marsh signed only days before the Centenary Test.

As they walked out together at the MCG, Marsh said : 'Enjoy it, mate. It'll be the last one we'll play on this ground.' Chappell feigned innocence, but Marsh retorted : 'You must know what I'm talking about. I've signed – haven't you ?'

Most of the Australians joined up before or during the Centenary Test, yet nothing leaked through, either to me or – to my knowledge – any of the other English players.

When we met I spelled out my requests to Mr Packer then sat back while he made the most extraordinary counter-proposal I have ever heard.

As England captain, recently having completed a successful four-month tour and with an Ashes series soon to follow, it came as more than a shock to be propositioned with a plan that basically involved being bought up for a commercial purpose. There could be no hasty decisions. I needed time to think and took it.

In the week that followed I tried to approach the offer from every angle, consider every possibility and take advice from as many trusted sources as possible – the accent had to be on trusted, for Packer's first action had been to demand absolute secrecy, whether I accepted the offer or not. I gave him my word.

I drafted a list in my mind of pros and cons, roughly reproduced here :

Pros

1 Being captain of England has never been a secure position for anyone, and, although the job was precious to me, I had promised never to subject myself to the treatment suffered by Mike Denness. This could be the chance to bow out while still on top.

2 I had always said, and still felt, that I did not want to go on with the seven-days-a-week grind of English first-class cricket beyond a maximum age of 32.

3 It had long been an ambition to finish my career in England by devoting a season or two to Sussex alone. They had given me my

opportunities in England and until then I had had little chance to repay them. A spell without international commitments would allow me that privilege – and, as far as I knew, Packer's plan fitted perfectly. Sussex also knew that this was my intention.

4 Australia appealed to me and my family. Donna and I had already touched on the possibility of living in Sydney at some future stage and the chance that this contract might hurry our decision did not disturb me at all.

5 Packer's offer included a guarantee of a job with his organization and a ladder to climb given that I was able to justify my ability in what amounted to a totally new world and challenge. This prospect, combined with the money he was offering for the cricket side of things, gave me a long-term security that was difficult to reject.

6 After a week's thought I was convinced that the scheme would be to the ultimate benefit of the game itself and every first-class cricketer. The process would not be swift and might need patience and careful handling. But, I believed, everyone stood to benefit.

Cons

1 I was almost certain to be sacked as England captain if I joined up. That went against the grain. Nobody likes being sacked from anything and I particularly resented the possibility of being ditched by my country just when I believed we had begun to build a powerful team.

2 The cricket authorities were bound to be severely jolted when news of the plan finally broke. If they acted hastily, cricket could be harmed in the short term.

3 Although I believed my commitment to Sussex would be unaffected, I conceded that signing for Packer would probably mean the end of my career as an England player – after more than fifty consecutive Tests.

4 Reaction to the scheme, through the media, was certain to be violent. If I signed I would be pilloried and, however phlegmatic I had become about press criticism, nobody relishes the inevitability of it all.

It was not an easy decision and those who have cynically assumed that I jumped at the sight of the cheque are talking nonsense. But the final two 'pros' convinced me that to sign for Packer was the right course. It *did* offer me undoubted security and I was sure that cricketers down the scale would benefit from it all eventually.

Of the disadvantages, I was worried least by the thought that the authorities were in for a shock. Quite simply, I believed it was overdue. They needed something like this to accelerate their progress towards a more business-like approach to the game.

It took another two meetings with Packer before I eventually signed and, by the time my mind was made up, very few ramifications had escaped my notice. I was even perfectly well aware that a court case was a strong possibility.

The captaincy of the World team was offered to me soon after my acceptance and I was pleased to take it. By now I was more sure of myself and willing to become involved in the organization of the project. So, when I was told that Austin Robertson, an aide of Packer, was scheduled for a trip to South Africa and the West Indies to recruit players, I intervened.

My reasoning was that cricketers were quite likely to be put on their guard by a businessman offering vast sums of money for what amounted to desertion however justifiable. What they needed was one of their own breed, another player, to explain the advantages and counter them with the potential pitfalls. Packer agreed, and I was soon bound for the West Indies – not, as many people later wrote, as a leader recruiting mercenaries, but as an adviser who could explain the whole thing in cricketers' language.

Back in England, I put similar proposals to Derek Underwood, Alan Knott and John Snow and left them to do their own thinking. By now the season was starting, yet still there was nothing appearing in the papers to suggest that the press had a sniff of the plans.

A story did appear in a Johannesburg newspaper, related to the scheme but unsupported by statements, and I hear that after all attempts to substantiate the article had been met with silence, English journalists in general gave up.

It had to come out eventually, of course, and it was fitting – yet completely unplanned – that the news broke on the weekend of my first major party at our home in Hove.

Donna and I had experienced a tremendously hospitable ten years in Sussex and we decided that a party would be a good way of showing some gratitude. We planned it for the Saturday evening of the Australians' visit to Hove and invited all the players. A marquee was pitched in our garden and, in later newspaper articles, it was referred to as 'the circus big top'.

On the Monday morning every newspaper carried the story, most of them on the front page. The comments did not begin until the following day and then they were much as expected – harsh, anti, and in some cases wildly inaccurate. I did not deny anyone their right to an opinion, nor did their views upset me, but I was angered by the reports which blatantly had their facts wrong.

I was called a bandit and a pirate and labelled greedy and selfish. Yet none of that hurt me so much as the references to my supposed wealth, presumably drawn from the fact that I lived in a big house and drove a Jaguar. The mortgage and the company who loaned me a car were forgotten.

It was nothing new for me to be the target for press attacks, however, and this was a case when I was helped by my past. But while I was capable of being philosophical, others were hit harder by a campaign that approached the victimization stage.

Meetings at Lord's naturally followed. So did a major press conference, at which – for the first time in my life – I experienced the odd sensation of knowing that many of my listeners did not believe a word of what I was saying. They had made up their own minds on the issue and no explanations from me were going to sway them.

When I insisted that cricket would benefit in the long term they stared and muttered as if I was a creature from another planet. Not many months later, though, my predictions began to come true, with the intervention of people like David Evans and the acceptance of the Cornhill deal that not only gave England players £1000 a Test but also ploughed money through the game at all levels. There was more to come – and none of it would have arrived in such haste but for Packer.

By the time Packer himself arrived in England his detractors were beginning to paint lurid verbal pictures of this ogre who was set on destroying cricket – and I suppose his appearance did little to moderate their ravings. Packer is a big, brash, aggressive Australian, who doesn't suffer fools gladly, and the cartoonists had a ball with his belligerent profile.

To meet him, however, is to be impressed. Much of his tycoon image as the tough and thirsty Aussie gives a false impression of a man who drinks coke and can be as soft as anyone's grandmother.

He is an exciting man, because he has such huge influence. But he is also thoroughly human. I suggest that most of those who have made him out to be an unscrupulous villain have never met him. I like him as a person and I don't feel obliged to make that statement because I work for him. If I didn't like him, I would say nothing at all.

His interest in cricket as a commercial concern was occasioned purely by the fact that Test cricket commands high television ratings. The game is healthy and it reflects in its worldwide appeal. A man like Packer does not just sit back and speculate on these facts – he acts. And, if the authorities will not at least attempt to accommodate him, he will take things into his own hands.

But, while the whole operation was set off by a fight over Australian television rights, it then expanded at an alarming rate to involve the careers and futures of dozens of men, me included.

So why, I have often been asked, was the plan not taken to the authorities instead of all the secrecy. My answer is that showing our hand would have defeated the object. A confrontation was necessary to force the authorities to put their own house in order. If they had accepted Packer's idea but organized the series themselves, everything would have gone on as before – with valuable money being turned away from the game.

Many believe I was deceitful and selfish, but I never saw it that way. I had certain regrets, and I certainly felt a twinge for people like Alec Bedser, who perhaps had grounds for thinking I had let him down.

But the way I saw the potential benefits of the plan, it would have been far more selfish if I had rejected the offer, carried on as England captain and effectively fought against something that I believed to be good.

My biggest wrench was the sacrifice of the England captaincy when I was on the threshold of my great remaining ambition in the game – to lead an Ashes-winning side. My sacking was not unexpected, but, even as I waited for the decision on a Friday afternoon at Lord's, I knew I was not going to like it.

The summer of '77 still holds a lot of pleasure for me, however. I had the compensation of knowing that I had played a significant part in putting England on the way back and I was proud still to be able to go out and give my all to another captain in a situation which I had created for myself. Some, I believe, would have felt too sour to go on.

All the English 'Packer signings' were included in the first Test of the series, the Jubilee occasion at Lord's. A number of critics had suggested that I, for one, should not have been picked, so the 91 I scored in our second innings of a drawn match gave me enormous satisfaction.

England won the next three matches to regain the Ashes in positive, triumphant fashion that reflected great credit on my successor, Mike Brearley. But there were many heroes in a united team effort, the most notable perhaps being Geoff Boycott, who returned belatedly but victoriously to the England side, and Bob Willis, who completed his transition into a world-class quick bowler.

Australia went home unhappily, their team about to divide for what was to be the most extraordinary winter of cricket the world has ever seen.

As for me, perhaps Test cricket had seen me off at the right time. I had six unforgettable seasons, four England tours and more memories than I could ever satisfactorily record.

But I'm not the type who wants to go on playing county cricket into his forties. While I can never fully repay the debt I owe to the game that has made me, I didn't intend to be dragged into middle age as a steadily deteriorating cricketer. Life means more to me than that. Besides I did also give the game my everything.

14

Packing up

For the next year Greig's life continued to be torrid, often turbulent. He was accused of many things, but whatever else his detractors accused him of, they never had the satisfaction of seeing him lose face. It has always been a feature of Greig's life that, whatever decision he reaches, it will be pursued and supported unfailingly to an end result – good or bad. So, although there were times when he doubted his own wisdom, Greig battled unceasingly both for the success of World Series and for an eventual peace agreement with the cricket authorities. Only when both materialized, and cricketers around the world suddenly began to find their pay packets growing, did a little of the acrimony cease. John Arlott, for one, called Greig a 'prophet without honour', as so much of what he had initially predicted had now come true. But, for Greig, it was not achieved without pain.

Leaving England, and all our friends and memories, was not an easy thing to do. But the decision to go was made, quite suddenly, one July afternoon in 1978. My mind was made up, not by the pressure of public feeling against me, but because I saw a blatant instance of victimization against my 4-year-old daughter. That, I could not take.

Up to this point my family had not been directly affected by the furore. Naturally, they had felt for me as the abuse appeared to increase in intensity almost daily, but the stirrers who seemed to delight in making my life unpleasant had at least not transferred their attentions to my wife and children. Until, that is, I went to collect Samantha from school one day.

She was attending a good school quite close to our home and was very happy there. Jonathan, a tremendous youngster, was probably her best friend, but she was also very close to a lovely little girl in her class. They spent endless happy hours together, both in our home and hers, and I had, on numerous occasions, driven round to collect Samantha after a day's play.

It was a practice in the school to hand out birthday party invitations through the class teacher. Samantha had had the entire class to her party and was now looking forward to her friend's big day.

The day for invitations arrived and I was waiting at the school for Samantha. Her friend's mother was a few yards away and we had already exchanged greetings when the two girls came skipping out of class, hand in hand, and joined the queue to collect the invitations. When it was her turn Samantha held out her hand, only to hear the teacher say, 'Sorry, Samantha, there doesn't appear to be one for you.' Her friend quickly said, 'Don't be silly, there must be one,' and ran over to her mother to tell her she had forgotten Samantha's invitation.

To my utter amazement, the mother simply said, 'She's not invited.' I have never been so hurt in my life. I took three strides towards Samantha, who jumped into my arms, tears running down her face.

I would not have minded if that woman had said to my face that she did not agree with what I had done to cricket – even to the point of saying she thought I was a disgrace. But to take out her feelings on two tiny, unsuspecting girls was surely unforgivable. I felt physically sick, and from that moment on my life in England was finished.

To be honest, the crunch had been coming for some time. My future, and the future of my family, now lay in Australia. We knew that, had accepted it as inevitable and also as exciting. As ever, when a new challenge looms on the horizon, my feet were itchy and my impatience uncontrollable.

From the moment I signed for WSC it had crossed my mind that I should resign as England captain. I had dismissed the thought because there was always the possibility, however slight, that peace might not be far away. After all, it had been Packer's inability to win the exclusive television rights which had led to the concept and, if he had somehow achieved that goal, WSC might never have seen the light of day.

I left any new moves to the establishment and sat tight, heeding the prophetic advice of Kerry that, 'If this keeps going the way it is now, we could all end up in court, and anything you say could be used.' Life was not easy, as I was constantly followed by press cameramen trying to catch me off guard. One even trained his camera on the front door of my home, while, every now and then, his colleague would knock. Their aim was clearly to send back film of me slamming the door in a reporter's face. They were disappointed.

The realization that I was no longer England captain was bitter. I had treasured the job more than most people could possibly imagine and, if that initial summit meeting at Lord's had been successful, it might well have still been mine. But, like so many things in life, if counts for nothing. I had made my decision and I had to accept the bitter consequences.

Rather more surprising to me at this stage, in mid-1977, had been an immediate move within Sussex to get rid of me. I was not going to make that easy for them and refused to resign. There were similar rumblings around Kent, but few people seriously expected them to dispense with Knott, Underwood, Asif Iqbal – and later Bob Woolmer, one of the additional signings, when the concept grew.

The possibility that we would all end up in court became near certainty during the Third Test of that 1977 series against Australia at Nottingham. It was an extraordinary period, with news of David Evans's incentive schemes being broken in the London press only hours after the WSC boat had been slightly rocked by Jeff Thomson withdrawing from his contract. His release was smoothed by a previous contract signed with a Brisbane radio station, which was dependent on his availability for the national side. How he had been so foolish as to sign conflicting contracts I cannot imagine, but his withdrawal was greeted ecstatically by our opponents.

Thomson was hailed as a saviour of the establishment cause and received an enormous ovation from the Trent Bridge crowd when he went out to bat. It was the first dent in what had apparently become rather solid armour, but I did not see it as a cue for panic.

Three days later Alvin Kallicharran also withdrew, but I lost no sleep at all over that. He was one of the many later signings

F

when it was decided to make the tournament a triangular one, involving Australia, the West Indies and a World XI. This had necessitated more players from England to augment the world squad, and I had opted for Dennis Amiss and Woolmer.

Later that season, however, I helped to talk Bob Willis and Derek Randall out of signing a WSC contract. I saw no point in either man making the change, now that so much extra money was being offered to Test players, and Willis also had a potentially lucrative benefit from Warwickshire approaching. I said nothing about this at the time, and my involvement in their decisions was never mentioned. With hindsight, perhaps I should have told the story, but I chose to withhold it.

At the end of that Test, J. P. Sport Pty Ltd, the company headed by Kerry Packer, Paul Hogan, John Cornell and Austin Robertson, issued writs in the High Court in England against the Test and County Cricket Board and the International Cricket Conference to prevent either body from banning any of the WSC players. They issued another writ against David Lord, who managed both defectors, Thomson and Kallicharran.

Mike Procter, John Snow and myself joined with J. P. Sport in their action against both the TCCB and the ICC as it became more and more apparent that the knives were out to such an extent that WSC players were facing a total ban. To us, that was restriction of trade and in England that is treated seriously.

The hearing, before Mr Justice Slynn, took the entire afternoon of the day following the completion of the Test, with the result to be known the next day. The two actions against the governing bodies were refused, but the judge accepted an undertaking that no players would be banned until the dispute had been fully tried in court. The court, however, granted a seven-day injunction against David Lord, restraining him from inducing players to break their contracts with J. P. Sport.

Back in Sydney, meanwhile, Packer was issuing writs against Australian cricket authorities for the same reason. Writs were the order of the day, as Kerry stuck to his word and supported his players to the hilt.

At this stage, any number of secret meetings were being held all over England, for I believe most of those involved, in whatever capacity, would have welcomed peace. Personally, I had meetings with both Bernie Coleman and Raman Subba-Row, two members of the TCCB executive for whom I have considerable respect.

Nothing, however, could halt the progress towards the first real test of strength in the High Court, and it was as we prepared ourselves for what would inevitably be a long and unpleasant case that the awareness that my Test career was, in all probability, over really got through to me.

I have to confess I found that hard to cope with. While my life revolved around lawyers and statements, the England team were readying themselves for the winter tour of Pakistan and New Zealand. Mike Brearley and his players were going through the traditional procedures of meeting at Lord's, being measured for tour uniforms and generally building up spirit and morale for the trip. I felt lost not being among them. It had been part of my life for so long.

But I did have motivation, and a prime consideration was the winning of the court case, not only for the players involved, but for Kerry Packer himself. Each one of us wanted to support him in the same way he had supported us.

There was a certain amount of self-preservation in my attitude, too. I had put my name and position on the line and, despite the occasional injuries to my pride, I had never wavered from the belief that all would eventually be well . . . for everyone.

I had come to realize just how much muscle the national Boards could wield – small wonder they had players virtually shivering in their shoes for so many years. But the strongest man of all was Packer. His intense optimism knew no bounds. If there were any queries or problems, his comment was always, 'I'll fix it' – and it meant just that. A remarkable man.

When the case finally began, I could not help but be impressed by the drama and excitement of the court-room. There was the judge, Mr Justice Slade, all alone with the responsibility of a decision that was to affect so many people, perhaps even change the basis on which cricket had operated for more than a century. I sat in awe of this man, day in, day out.

Apart from admiring the brilliance of our counsel, Robert Alexander QC and Andrew Merrit QC, I then grew to find the entire proceedings thoroughly boring, and occasionally unsavoury. I had never been in a court before, let alone in the witness box, and I was lost. I had no idea of court etiquette. I had to keep quiet for periods far longer than ever before . . . and I couldn't smoke! It was very hard work.

Another aspect to emerge from this sorry affair was the straining of some long-standing friendships and the destruction of others. I well remember walking towards the court one day as Alec Bedser approached. Under normal circumstances we would have walked across a street to greet each other. Here, that was not possible. It was as if he wanted to be a stranger, and I have never been cut out to be like that. To feel that I could not talk to such a good friend as Alec, just because he was 'on the other side', really hurt me. I realize there was no alternative, but to me a friend is a friend, no matter what the prevailing circumstances.

As my turn in the witness box approached, I found it far more frightening than waiting to bat in a Test match. For some reason I felt like a criminal, especially when I was first attacked by the opposition counsel. My initial impulse was to tell all our opposition to go and jump in the lake. All reasoning disappeared, despite the fact that we were bringing the action. It became a battle, with the opposition trying to pull me apart and Alexander protecting me. It was a gruelling exercise. For almost two days I stood there, the centre of a thrust and parry tactical battle I likened to a Test match – and which, to me, was every bit as important.

I must admit I was glad when my part was over. But I was, quite innocently, about to run head-first into more trouble.

Geoff Boycott, I gathered, was due to appear as an establishment witness early the following week. Boycott had been outspoken against several previous England captains and selectors, yet here he was about to speak virtually on their behalf. It appealed to my sense of humour, and I looked forward to Boycott facing the kind of ordeal I had just gone through.

By coincidence a sports trade fair, which I had hoped to attend, was taking place at Birmingham that weekend. As a director of St Peters, makers of cricket equipment, I had wanted to represent the company but the court case made it impossible. I happened to know, however, that Boycott, who was also on the staff of St Peters at that time, would be going. So I phoned him and asked if he would bring some bats down to London for me.

I added, 'By the way, Geoff, we're looking forward to throwing some mud at you when you give evidence.' It was said more in jest than anything, but under the circumstances it was not a bright thing to do. Boycott told his solicitor, who reported me to the judge, claiming that I had intimidated a witness, or words to that effect. I soon found out that this was no climate for by-play when the judge reprimanded me, adding that I would be in contempt of court if I repeated such an action.

My mind went back over previous conversations with Geoffrey Boycott. As England captain, and a selector, I had always wanted him in my side, and never believed that any previous behaviour, such as his long self-imposed Test exile, should be considered. We were having a hard time of it in my early Tests as captain, and all I was concerned with was gathering a squad capable of beating India and winning the Centenary Test on our 1976–77 tour.

I had two meetings with Boycott before that trip, and even offered him the vice-captaincy. I had no right to do that without consulting my co-selectors, but I was confident that I was doing the right thing. Boycott told me that, if he was available, he would let me know. I'm still waiting.

Boycott has made some weird decisions over the years, but I found this inexplicable. I had offered to smooth his path back, and he ignored it. When I arrived at the tour selection meeting, incidentally, the first question I asked was, 'Is Boycott available?' Charlie Elliott, the former Test umpire, now a selector, replied in the negative, and I knew I had not only lost the argument, but a great player. Later, Boycott was to say that he had made himself available, maintaining he had told Elliott so. To this day, I don't know who to believe.

Just before the Centenary Test, Boycott also had a meeting with Kerry Packer in Sydney. I am told he shook hands and agreed to play in WSC. When Austin Robertson gave him a contract, however, he had changed his mind.

Having lost Boycott for that tour, despite doing everything possible to get him involved, I missed his help and his sound, tactical advice. But I believe, as many others do, that he was too selfish to be a leader. He could have made a bigger and better contribution to the game had he been content to stick to his batting. Time was to prove that right.

Boycott eventually did get the England captaincy, albeit by

default, when Brearley broke his arm in Pakistan, early in 1978. But he did not intend to stop there. With the leadership in his grasp at last, he launched into a tirade against WSC players, labelling them 'disloyal, traitors . . . have bat, will travel'. I saw red. It was a case of someone in a very fragile glass house throwing stones, for I will never forget that Boycott was commentating during the Centenary Test, when his rightful place was on the field with us. Was that not disloyal?

From my base in Sydney, I wrote an article, stating that, 'Boycott has the uncanny knack of being where fast bowlers aren't,' and therefore had no right to criticize others who had been through thick and thin. My comment lit the fuse for more trouble, as, under TCCB regulations, I was supposed to receive clearance for all public statements.

Did Boycott get his comments cleared by either the TCCB or the tour manager Ken Barrington? I suspect he didn't. Both his comments and mine were personal views which went impulsively into print. But what happened? To Boycott, nothing at all. To me, a two-month suspension from county cricket.

Sussex were now virtually obliged to relieve me of the captaincy. Arnold Long took over and, while I waited for the result of the court case and spent my suspension playing a few club games for Brighton and Hove, it was my view that the Sussex club as a whole were disappointingly weak.

I had always had a good relationship with the chairman, Tony Crole-Rees, and believed he was doing a fine job for the county. But I also believed that he was against both the way the TCCB had handled the Packer affair and the subsequent court case – and should have said so. But, like so many others at the time, he became a 'yes man' to the power of Lord's. I was dismayed, and I wrote to tell him so.

When my ban was lifted, I returned to Hove, and was horrified by what I saw. All the old, bad habits had crept back into the side . . . the cliques which banded senior players together and cast out the young and inexperienced to fend for themselves. An impossible and totally undesirable situation was back.

During my time as captain, I had tried to change all that, not dining with the same players all the time, but switching and changing so that I came to know and understand each player personally. The same problems had been apparent at Middlesex until Mike Brearley brought everyone into the fold as one – and that is the only way in which a team can function happily. I brought this to the attention of Crole-Rees and Long, but they could not – or would not – see it. I was getting more edgy every day.

It was shortly after this that the WSC birthday party episode brought everything to a head. The following morning, I went to the County Ground and once more noticed the huddles – seniors with seniors, juniors making their own arrangements – and I knew that I would only make matters worse by staying, because I would have to say something. I had to get out.

I phoned Donna and asked her to join me for coffee at the ground. I told her everything that was irking me. 'Let's go to Australia now,' I suggested. 'The kids are young enough, so why wait?' Donna agreed. I walked into the office of Stanley Allen, the Sussex secretary, told him that I was resigning and would not leave the office until I had both signed the resignation and obtained release from my contract.

I also explained everything to Stanley, because I owed him at least that. One of the regrets we were to have at the decision made that day was leaving the many genuine friends we had made over the years. It had been an alarming experience, finding out who our real friends were. But, when things became nasty, they stood out like oases in the desert. So many we had counted as friends just fell by the wayside when it seemed possible they would become unpopular by siding with me. The true friends, those whose support never faltered, were hard to leave, and we will never forget them. Stanley was one of the best. Although his hands were somewhat tied by his position with Sussex, he still found time to prove his support with the great friendship he has always shown.

Two more, whose help when the going got tough I could never really express in words, were Alan Caffyn and his wife, Anne. Alan and his family own a garage chain and, as I had driven one of his cars for years, I had many reasons to be grateful to him.

Donna, who also left behind three wonderful girl friends, accepted the decision quite happily, although I know she must have hated leaving the home into which she had put so much work. I believe she had been aware of the possibility that we might have to leave ever since I told her of Packer's plans, way back in March of 1977, an apparent eternity ago. She had built that home with loving care, making countless improvements in a relatively short time, and we had had every intention of enjoying the fruits of her labours for as long as we lived. Yet, to her immense credit, Donna never uttered a word of complaint. She understood her support was vital to me, and throughout everything she has been nothing short of magnificent.

I rang Kerry that night to explain my decision, and his normal encouragement came through from 12000 miles distance. 'The tickets will be waiting for you in the morning,' was his reply. So there it was, the choice made. We were leaving England behind, probably for good. I was now a Packer player, and a Packer employee, through and through.

15
Packer and beyond

World Series Cricket, in its independent form, operated for just two seasons. They were mixed seasons for Greig; his form was often poor, certainly by his own previous big-match standards, yet he was able to enjoy the sight of WSC gaining public acceptance, both at the gate and through the television medium, in its second season. There was, however, far more to it all than dressing up in brightly coloured kit and playing with a white ball. . . .

One very serious comment from Derek Underwood, as he finally signed the contract which made him a World Series player, summed up the whole thing for me. 'Be it on your own head,' he said.

I have no regrets, none whatsoever, about my part in WSC. I went into it with my eyes wide open, and tried to ensure that others did the same. Despite that fact, there were many hours of pain, many hours of soul-searching worry and uneasiness.

The uneasiness began soon after my return from the Centenary Test. Flushed with the excitement of the tour, and now the quite bewildering new thrills offered by Packer, I was keen to have a long discussion with my father. The opportunity was granted in the most unexpected manner, as I found myself guest of honour of the television programme *This is Your Life.*

Everyone was there – my parents, Tackies, our African gardener, my kindergarten teacher, all the England team – and I had known nothing whatever about it. It was a moving honour, but, as the accolades flowed through the half-hour show, I kept thinking to myself : 'Oh dear, if only they knew what was to come.' It was a rather sickening feeling, but one I could do absolutely nothing about.

The certainty that I would be crucified for my part in WSC

never deterred me, but the fact that I was also mocked for having the audacity to suggest that the plight of all players would subsequently improve I found very unfair. So it is with considerable satisfaction that I can now reflect on recent events.

The Test fees of England's players have risen 600 per cent since the advent of WSC and, on the last tour of Australia, in 1979–80, Mike Brearley's squad earned up to £10000 a man. When I started with England I received £1500 a tour – and only got £3500 for my final trip, to India and Australia in 1976–77. County players have also reaped the benefit, despite all the scepticism. Nowadays, the minimum basic wage for a capped player is £4750, a good deal more than I received from Sussex when I was captain of county and country.

Some of the hierarchy at Lord's have suggested that it would have happened anyway. Rubbish! If that were true, it would have taken ten years, not a matter of months.

Looking back, however, I still marvel that the project ever got off the ground at all. For one of my first tasks, having left England to settle in Australia and work for Packer, was to visit WSC's Melbourne venue, VFL Park. It boasts a capacity of 100000, but had been used purely for Australian Rules football and I had never heard of the place – but I will never forget it now, after my initial sighting as our helicopter hovered over the ground. To my disbelief and dismay there was a huge hole in the centre of the playing area, with great piles of sand on the surrounds. It was impossible to envisage an international cricket pitch being in place and fit for use within a matter of weeks . . . the whole scheme, for an awful few minutes, seemed to be doomed to failure.

Behind the stand, however, was a hot-house with two pitches set in concrete casing, both of monstrous size. The exercise of moving the cases into the centre by hovercraft was just another revolutionary innovation, in keeping with everything else. History records that the hovercraft idea didn't work, because the cases were too heavy, so a crane was used instead. The wickets were ferried by rail to their central position, where the wires for heating were embedded. I was very involved with the planning in these early stages, but I found this an incredible feat. After that success, anything was possible.

One of the most interesting aspects was planning the television production. Where to place the cameras for the best angles, where to hold the interviews. Those involved in pulling together all that went out on Channel 9 did a superb job.

Kerry Packer was in his element, holding forth on so many subjects, all vital to the success of the operation. His energy knew no bounds, and I think he took it as a personal slight when precious few people turned up for the opening match.

I was quite sure there were more people in the V I P areas than in the stands. The V F L complex is so vast that it seemed there were no more than a dozen or so spectators in the ground, yet the cameras had been so strategically placed that, to watch on television, you would swear there were thousands.

There was a minor drama in the V I P dining-room on the opening day, and it showed Packer at his most resourceful. The food, at best, was poor, and Kerry was furious that his guests were being so poorly treated. Without a word he left the ground, filled his car boot with McDonald's hamburgers, then returned to pile them on the table.

A worried chef emerged to see the competition, his food untouched. Unsmilingly, he said, 'I think you are trying to tell me something.' From that day on, we enjoyed a daily banquet.

It would be unrealistic to deny that those early days were hard going. We had started from scratch and, as players, were not accustomed to making our own way. We were all used to managers on tour, to ensure that everything went according to a prearranged itinerary. Now we had to do everything and, although it was worrying at first, we set ourselves the criterion of deciding on the bad areas of previous tours and improving on them.

Kerry's enthusiasm was infectious. I had come to know the man extremely well and marvelled at his all-round expertise. His thirst for knowledge of cricket was insatiable. One morning in Perth I went to his room, as arranged, only to find he had already left for our ground at Gloucester Park. I found him working the roller, having already spent some time with John Maley, the groundsman, behind the hot-house wickets, wanting to know everything and, what is more, lend a hand.

His finger was on the pulse of everything, thanks sometimes to the famous 'red phone', a direct line to his television producer. It didn't matter if he was at the ground or in any of his offices, he would just pick up the red phone and ask, 'What's going on with that bloke on camera four?' and it would be fixed.

Watching Kerry operate and knowing how vital he was to the success of WSC made me recall the second Test against Australia in Manchester, during the 1977 series. I was called to the phone some two hours before play started. The caller introduced himself as representing a Melbourne newspaper and asked if I had heard the news. 'What news?' I asked. 'Kerry Packer has been killed in a car accident, on the way from Tullamarine Airport to Melbourne, along with three others.'

I was stunned, my heart beating like a drum. The caller asked for a comment, but I was too numb to think, or even speak. I had been a passenger with Kerry many times and knew him to be a pretty fast driver. It was quite possibly true. I asked the fellow to ring back in an hour.

My head was reeling and I felt sick at the very thought that Kerry was dead. I had come to like him immensely and, if the report was true, WSC was merely a memory . . . only Packer could make it work. I headed for the Australian dressing-room and told Greg Chappell. His initial reaction matched mine, although he said : 'Let's wait and see if it's confirmed.'

I went back down the corridor and, on impulse, rang Kerry's home number in Sydney. He answered the phone himself and a great wave of relief swept over me. I told him the story, to which he calmly replied, 'Well, I haven't, have I?' It was all a hoax, but it left me with the apprehensive feeling that the guts could drop out of the entire plan. Kerry Packer was not just the key, he was the whole house.

In many ways he is a patient man. He rated Alan Knott the ultimate pessimist and, as a result, spent hours allaying his fears, proving to the little wicketkeeper that it pays to be optimistic. Kerry should know that better than most.

When he rang me in Perth during a Super-Test against Australia with the news that we had won the High Court decision on all counts, he sounded no different in success from what he sounded like in times of high stress.

I admit to periods of depression in those early days, and Kerry would pick them up immediately. 'Come and have a drink,' he would say. It did not matter what time of day or night it might be, he knew I needed an ally to boost me, and he provided one.

One of the biggest disappointments to me during WSC was the attitude of Ian Chappell. Over the years the two of us have had more than our share of tussles, but they had mainly been captain to captain, with no nastiness attached. That was to change.

Packer's early edicts included a directive on dress. We were, he said, to look like representatives of a professional group. That did not upset me at all, as I have always believed in a smart uniform and consequently insisted on high standards. But Chappell was exactly the opposite. He opted for total abandonment of dress standards, just as he had done as Australia's captain before his retirement. Perhaps I am simply old-fashioned but I was not about to change and neither was he.

A travel uniform was devised and blazers were ordered with WSC buttons, but the concept was never adopted. That, I believe, was one of the few mistakes we made. It bugged me that we should travel anonymously, in some cases scruffily, while establishment tour teams invariably dressed in uniform smartness. But Chappell did not care at all – he would wear what he damn well pleased.

Chappell's outbursts eventually riled me. It started in Perth, during the first year of WSC. The World XI players had pointed out to the umpire that a spectator had caught the ball inside the boundary and that the stroke was therefore worth 4, not 6. The umpire agreed and altered his signal, whereupon Chappell raced on to the field, dressed in shorts and thongs, to demand of the umpire : 'Who is running this game, you or the South Africans?' It was a highly unprofessional attitude to take, particularly as we were all trying to sell WSC in those awkward teething days. But I expected better from Ian Chappell.

He became predictable. Every time the Australians lost, he would vent his feelings on me through a personal attack. He did, admittedly, have some justification on his side. I knew only too well that I was playing poorly and eventually, early in the second season, I dropped myself to the country circuit, which was virtually a second-eleven championship.

Armed with some success, I reinstated myself in the World side for the Super-Test final against the Australians at Sydney, in which we were successful. At the presentation ceremony, Chappell walked down the line of my players, shaking hands and saying,

'Well played.' When he reached me, he withheld his hand and made the quip, 'Your team has done it again.' To a degree he was right, but what is the point of carrying on like that? However, having had a go at Chappell, I should like to make it clear that I do have a tremendous amount of respect for his ability as a leader and a cricketer. He did get the best out of his players and one always knew exactly what he felt because he consistently spoke his mind.

If these were low points, there were also some memorable highs, none better than the first night match at the SCG, in November 1978. I flew down from Orange with Bob Woolmer, Dennis Amiss and our wives, and felt absolutely tired out as we approached the ground in Sydney. But I forgot all that as we parked and walked towards the upper deck of the Noble Stand, directly behind the arm. When we reached the landing and saw the massive crowd of more than 50000 choking the ground, I had tears in my eyes.

All the hard work had been worth it. WSC had been accepted. There were people everywhere, and now we had something to work on. I wondered fleetingly how many members of the Australian Board were watching. I wondered if they really believed it, or if they were cursing to each other on the phone and discussing how best to combat – or accept – it.

Kerry saw me from a distance. He, more than anyone else outside my family, knew how much I had put into it in terms of blood, sweat and tears, and he knew what this sight must mean to me. Calling me aside as I said, 'This is it,' Kerry replied, 'Yes, I think you're right,' in the same manner I had come to accept as quite normal. Deep down I think he may have felt quite triumphant that night, but, if he did, it certainly didn't show. It was almost as if he had always known it would happen.

Looking back on the whole lengthy episode, we made only one major mistake – and that was not signing the entire England side from the start. This would directly have involved the TCCB as much as the Australian Board and, I firmly believe, peace would have been achieved much faster. At the outset I am convinced it would have been easy to complete these signings, but, by the time we thought of it, it was too late.

But 'ifs', as I have said before, count for nothing. Life is like cricket – only facts and statistics prove a point. And, eventually, the point which mattered above all others is that the rift was closed. The war ended.

There was enormous relief on both sides when the hatchet was finally buried, ending the two most incredible years cricket has seen. Now, I suggest, it will be seen in years to come that the game in general is better off for it all.

Primarily, of course, the players have benefited, especially those from England, the West Indies and Pakistan, and the authorities have received the shake-up they undoubtedly needed.

In Australia the Board have resumed control, but now have the backing of professional marketing men who know what it takes to sell a product. This is something I advocated throughout my playing days, and I have no doubt that similar innovations will be made, to good effect, the world over.

From the public point of view, Australia, and to a lesser extent the West Indies, enjoyed WSC for the opportunity it gave them to see the world's best players, week in, week out. There was much talk of saturation, but that problem will exist, I am sure, in the short-term only. Spectators will only pay to see the best and, for those who could not attend WSC matches, the Channel Nine network gave hundreds of hours of classic television. The spectator had a feast – and, if the spectator is happy, the game is healthy.

To be frank, I doubt if WSC has made much difference to establishment administration, other than by forcing them to recognize and improve the plight of the player and, hopefully, realize that the game should be run on more businesslike lines. The structure of cricket organization is still much the same as before, but I am certain there will be changes. Sometime, in the not too distant future, highly professional and well-paid businessmen will run the administrative side of the game.

Cricket *is* big business now and, whether we like it or not, it has to be run that way. There are precious few, if any, successful operations run by honorary committees, and for too long cricket and cricketers bowed to these well-meaning but unqualified men, some of whom gained the label of 'gin-and-tonic set' and the reputation that they regarded nothing as more important than their own egos.

I would never suggest that all committee men have such faults, nor that there is no place for them in cricket. There is – and a very important one. But at the top, in the positions which really matter, efficient executives must take over – and, if they fail, face the sack in the same way that they would in any other business.

Above all, the aim must be to make cricket profitable and, with that profit, protect the present and secure the future.

The belief that our game was above rebellion has been proved wrong, but good management can alleviate the danger of industrial unrest. The treatment of players, and their rights as individuals, has been one of suppression for too long and it is fair to say that, where that principle has been applied in other forms of employment, an uprising was inevitable.

The formation of various players' unions will also prove beneficial, providing the players do not become militant. I have no doubt that, if cricketers are financially comfortable and allowed to make their points of view heard, there will be no further strife. The responsibility for peace rests with administrators and players equally – and, if one thing is certain, it is that the players can never take control. It would be a disaster.

Without the player there is no game; without the spectator there is no game. But without expert administration, the game will never prosper and could eventually fade. Cricket is not a charity and has to be geared to profitmaking. So, at the end of it all, I believe the split in the game was worthwhile for all the good that came from it.

Personally, after the years of unrest and upheaval, I have found contentment in the shape of a new challenge. As managing director of Lion Insurance Brokers I have a ladder to climb . . . thanks to Kerry Packer. For years I worried about what the future would hold, how to bridge that vitally important gap when I retired. Now that problem has been solved in a most exciting way.

I have done everything I ever wanted on the cricket field – and more than I ever reasonably expected. I thought I had achieved the ultimate when I played for England, but I was still more fortunate to be made captain. I worked hard to achieve those goals, and I am no different now. In truth, I am a restless man, never really happy unless I have a target, a material ambition to spur me on.

Having toured the world on many occasions, and met so many

marvellous people, I am at peace with myself and, equally important, I come home to my family each night.

For me, happiness is life's key word and it revolves around Donna, Samantha and Mark. The kids are growing fast and we are now enjoying being part of that together. Happiness also revolves around real friends, and those we have found.

The challenges are all there, just as Kerry promised they would be. If over the years I have hurt anyone I am sorry. At 33 not many people can say in all honesty that they have never been happier. But I can.

Career Record

Compiled by Bill Frindall

NOTES

Greig was the first England player to take five wickets in an innings and score a century in the same Test (v. West Indies at Bridgetown, 1973–74). At Port-of-Spain later in the same rubber, he became the first to take eight wickets in an innings for England against West Indies. Greig remains the only player to score 3000 runs and take 100 wickets for England in official Tests.

ALL FIRST CLASS MATCHES

BATTING AND FIELDING   * not out

Season	Venue	M	I	NO	HS	Runs	Avge	100	50	Ct
1965–6	SA	1	2	–	37	42	21·00	–	–	2
1966	E	2	2	1	26	51	51·00	–	–	–
1967	E	33	56	3	156	1299	24·50	2	8	29
1967–8	P/I	3	5	–	106	195	39·00	1	1	5
1968	E	32	54	4	117	1305	26·10	1	8	28
1968–9	SA	6	9	–	94	250	27·77	–	2	3
1969	E	27	44	3	104	1130	27·56	1	7	15
1969–70	SA	4	6	1	48*	141	28·20	–	–	2
1969–70	WI	3	4	–	65	145	36·25	–	2	3
1970	E	26	46	4	113*	1008	24·00	1	7	31
1970–71	SA	6	10	1	73	147	16·33	–	1	9
1971	E	27	50	4	113	1242	27·00	2	5	31
1971–2	A	10	16	2	70	525	37·50	–	6	1
1971–2	SA	4	6	–	29	80	13·33	–	–	7
1972	E	16	27	4	112	1031	44·82	1	9	14
1972–3	R	2	4	1	39	85	28·33	–	–	1
1972–3	I/C/P	13	21	3	148	826	45·88	1	6	16
1973	E	17	27	2	139	721	28·84	2	2	14
1973–4	WI	9	14	1	148	665	51·15	3	1	12
1974	E	18	28	1	106	669	24·77	1	4	24
1974–5	SA	3	5	1	45	143	35·75	–	–	3
1974–5	A/NZ	14	22	2	167*	934	46·70	2	7	19
1975	E	20	37	1	226	1699	47·19	5	8	16
1976	E	18	32	3	116	765	26·37	1	5	19
1976–7	I/C	11	16	2	162*	633	45·21	2	4	12
1976–7	A	2	4	–	41	72	18·00	–	–	4
1977	E	18	24	–	91	735	30·62	–	4	21
1978	E	5	8	1	32	122	17·42	–	–	4
Totals		350	579	45	(226)	16,660	31·19	26	97	345

HUNDREDS (26)

For England (8)

148 v.	India	Bombay, 1972–3
139	New Zealand	Nottingham, 1973
148	West Indies	Bridgetown, 1973–4
121	West Indies	Georgetown, 1973–4
106	India	Lord's, 1974
110	Australia	Brisbane, 1974–5
116	West Indies	Leeds, 1976
103	India	Calcutta, 1976–7

For Sussex (14)

156 v.	Lancashire *(on Championship debut)*	Hove, 1967
123	Gloucestershire	Bristol, 1967
117	Gloucestershire	Hove, 1968
104	Warwickshire	Birmingham, 1969
113*	Kent	Tunbridge Wells, 1970
112	Hampshire	Portsmouth, 1971
113	Kent	Eastbourne, 1971
112	Worcestershire	Hove, 1972
139	Gloucestershire	Hove, 1973
121	Oxford University	Oxford, 1975
226	Warwickshire	Hastings, 1975
129*	Australians	Hove, 1975
147	Worcestershire	Worcester, 1975
103	Kent	Hove, 1975

For MCC (3)

100* v.	Trinidad	Port-of-Spain, 1973–4
167*	W. Australia	Perth, 1974–5
162*	W. Zone	Poona, 1976–7

For International XI (1)

106 v.	Chief Minister's XI	Madras, 1967–8

BOWLING † 8-ball overs

Season	Venue	O	M	R	W	Avge	5wI	10wM
1965–6	SA	43	14	97	2	48·50	–	–
1966	E	46	13	145	6	24·16	–	–
1967	E	669·5	164	1777	67	26·52	3	1
1967–8	P/I	40	12	104	5	20·80	–	–
1968	E	663·3	153	1972	55	35·85	–	–
1968–9	SA	271·4	76	712	25	28·48	1	1
1969	E	543·5	130	1629	69	23·60	2	–
1969–70	SA	147·4	42	364	19	19·15	2	1
1969–70	WI	41	8	107	4	26·75	–	–
1970	E	528·2	108	1634	59	27·69	2	–
1970–71	SA	172·5	38	501	9	55·66	–	–
1971	E	799·4	168	2239	77	29·07	4	1
1971–2	A	172·6†	23	664	26	25·53	1	–
1971–2	SA	141·2	34	333	25	13·32	3	1
1972	E	468·2	130	1102	41	26·87	2	1
1972–3	R	67	7	227	2	113·50	–	–
1972–3	I/C/P	329·1	89	759	29	26·17	1	–
1973	E	414·3	88	1180	38	31·05	–	–
1973–4	WI	277·1	57	766	30	25·53	3	1
1974	E	551·5	123	1677	55	30·49	1	–
1974–5	SA	94	16	292	15	19·46	1	–
1974–5	A/NZ	367·2†	63	1421	50	28·42	3	1
1975	E	621·5	152	1871	56	33·41	2	–
1976	E	442·5	96	1319	36	36·63	2	–
1976–7	I/C	{ 172 1† }	33	515	12	42·91	–	–
1976–7	A	29†	3	124	3	45·66	–	–
1977	E	319·2	90	850	35	24·28	–	–
1978	E	111	21	321	6	53·50	–	–
Totals		{ 7977·4 +570† }	1951	24,702	856	28·85	33	

TEN OR MORE WICKETS IN A MATCH (8)

For England (2)

13–156 v. West Indies   Port of-Spain, 1973–4
          (record match analysis in any Test in the West Indies)
10–149   New Zealand   Auckland, 1974–5

For Sussex (3)

10–79 v. Hampshire   Hove, 1967
11–81   Kent   Tunbridge Wells, 1971
11–46   Kent   Hastings, 1972

For Border (2)

10–117 v. OFS   Bloemfontein, 1968–69
10–84   N.E. Transvaal East London, 1969–70

For Eastern Province (1)

10–43   v. W. Province   Port Elizabeth, 1971–2

SIX OR MORE WICKETS IN AN INNINGS (12)

For England (2)

6–164 v. West Indies   Bridgetown, 1973–4
8–86   West Indies   Port-of-Spain, 1973–4

For Sussex (8)

6–45   v. Hampshire   Hove, 1967
8–25   Gloucestershire Hove, 1967
7–74   Nottinghamshire Hove, 1970
8–42   Kent   Tunbridge Wells, 1971
6–42   Kent   Eastbourne,1971
6–20   Kent   Hastings, 1972
6–50   Middlesex   Lord's, 1974
6–32   Surrey   Hove, 1976

For the Rest of the World (1)

6–30   v. Australians   Adelaide, 1971–2

For Border (1)

6–65   v. OFS   Bloemfontein, 1968–9

HAT-TRICK (1)

For Eastern Province

         v. Natal   Port Elizabeth, 1971–2

TEST MATCHES

BATTING AND FIELDING

Season	Opponents	M	I	NO	HS	Runs	Avge	100	50	Ct
1972	Australia	5	9	1	62	288	36·00	–	3	8
1972–3	India	5	8	2	148	382	63·66	1	2	9
1972–3	Pakistan	3	5	–	72	261	52·20	–	2	3
1973	New Zealand	3	5	–	139	216	43·20	1	1	1
1973	West Indies	3	5	–	44	122	24·40	–	–	5
1973–4	West Indies	5	9	–	148	430	47·77	2	–	7
1974	India	3	2	–	106	159	79·50	1	1	2
1974	Pakistan	3	4	–	37	90	22·50	–	–	11
1974–5	Australia	6	11	–	110	446	40·54	1	3	12
1974–5	New Zealand	2	1	–	51	51	51·00	–	1	1
1975	Australia	4	8	–	96	284	35·50	–	2	4
1976	West Indies	5	9	1	116	243	30·37	1	1	6
1976–7	India	5	8	–	103	342	42·75	1	2	5
1976–7	Australia	1	2	–	41	59	29·50	–	–	4
1977	Australia	5	7	–	91	226	32·28	–	2	9
Totals		58	93	4	(148)	3599	40·43	8	20	87

BOWLING   †8-ball overs

Season	Opponents	O	M	R	W	Avge	5wI	10wM
1972	Australia	162·3	44	398	10	39·80	–	–
1972–3	India	143·5	52	247	11	22·45	1	–
1972–3	Pakistan	78·2	10	255	6	42·50	–	–
1973	New Zealand	74·5	15	185	8	23·12	–	–
1973	West Indies	105·1	12	402	7	57·42	–	–
1973–4	West Indies	207·1	46	543	24	22·62	3	1
1974	India	70·1	16	176	6	29·33	–	–
1974	Pakistan	79·5	23	222	8	27·75	–	–
1974–5	Australia	167·5†	19	681	17	40·05	–	–
1974–5	New Zealand	50†	8	176	12	14·66	2	1
1975	Australia	97	23	322	8	40·25	–	–
1976	West Indies	98	15	336	5	67·20	–	–
1976–7	India	131	28	336	10	33·60	–	–
1976–7	Australia	14†	3	66	2	33·00	–	–
1977	Australia	77	25	196	7	28·00	–	–
Totals		{ 1324·5 +231·5†	339	4541	141	32·20	6	2

CAPTAINCY

Matches 14; wins 3 (all v. India); losses 5 (Australia 1, West Indies 3, India 1); draws 6 (Australia 3, West Indies 2, India 1). Won toss 6 times.

WORLD SERIES CRICKET RECORD
Compiled by Irving Rosenwater

1977–8

Super Tests

	Matches	Innings	Not out	Runs	Highest Score	Average
Batting	3	5	0	71	38	14·20
	Overs	Maidens		Runs	Wickets	Average
Bowling	67·4	6		283	7	40·42

International Cup

	Matches	Innings	Not out	Runs	Highest Score	Average
Batting	9	8	0	205	59	25·62
	Overs	Maidens		Runs	Wickets	Average
Bowling	28·3	1		195	5	39·00

1978–9

Super Tests

	Matches	Innings	Not out	Runs	Highest Score	Average
Batting	1	1	0	0	0	0
	Overs	Maidens		Runs	Wickets	Average
Bowling	1	0		7	0	0

International Cup

	Matches	Innings	Not out	Runs	Highest Score	Average
Batting	6	6	1	97	62	19·40
	Overs	Maidens		Runs	Wickets	Average
Bowling	15	1		67	1	67·00

Index

Abbas, Zaheer, 105
Acfield, David, 69
Ackerman, Hylton, 52, 94, 95–6
Afrikaans language, 34, 51
Alexander, Robert, QC, 161, 162
Allen, Stanley, 165
Amiss, Dennis, 71, 131, 138, 144, 148–9, 160, 172
Arlott, John, 157
Arnold, Geoff, 71, 79, 98
Arthur Gilligan's XI, 59
Australia:
   Centenary Test Match (1977), 148, 150, 151, 163, 164
   MCC Tour (1970–71), 77, 93–4
   MCC Tour (1974–5), 79, 80, 109–14
   MCC Tour (1976–7), 149–50, 163
   MCC Tour (1979–80), 168
   Rest of the World Tour (1970–71), 94–7
   Sheffield Shield, 123
   Waverley Club, 122, 123
   West Indies Tour (1975–6), 122, 124–5
   World Series Cricket, 157, 158, 159, 160, 167–73
   see also Test Matches in England

Bacher, Ali, 15, 16
Bailey, Trevor, 37
Bangalore, 148
Barbados, 109
Barlow, Eddie, 92
Barlow, Graham, 137, 146
Barnard, Christiaan, 11
Barrier Reef, 124

Barrington, Ken, 129, 131, 141, 164
Bedi, Bishen, 99, 135, 138, 141, 146
Bedser, Alec, 110, 117, 155, 162
Birrell, Harry, 141
Bombay, 101
Bond, Jack, 93
Border Schools, 51–2, 53
Boycott, Geoff, 108–9, 156, 162–4
Bradman, Sir Donald, 39, 94–6, 97
Brearley, Mike, 59, 107, 118, 127, 138, 156, 161, 164, 165, 168
Brisbane Test (1974–75), 110–12
British Lions, 87
Brown, David, 92
Brown, Tony, 105
Buss, Mike, 53, 55, 56, 66, 68, 104
Buss, Tony, 56, 57, 66, 68, 72, 93, 104

Calcutta (Eden Gardens):
   1972–3 Test, 101, 102
   1976–7 Test, 129–47
Caffyn, Anne and Alan, 165
Cambridge University cricket team, 69
Camp Cove, Sydney, 122, 123
Captain of England, Greig's appointment as, 28–9, 115–18, 124
Carr, Donald, 94, 102
Centenary Test Match, Australia (1977), 148, 150, 151, 163, 164
Chandrasekhar, B.S., 141
Chappell, Greg, 106, 120, 121, 150–51, 170

Chappell, Ian, 29, 112, 113, 120, 121, 125, 171–2
Close, Brian, 126
Coleman, Bernie, 161
Colonel Stevens' XI, 59
Compton, Denis, 38, 149
Cooper, Mrs Flo, 57, 70
Cooper, Graham, 66
Cooper, Henry, 86
Cornell, John, 160
Cottam, Bob, 118–19
Cowdrey, Colin, 37, 38, 39, 71, 75, 113
Crole-Rees, Tony, 164, 165
Currie Cup, 14, 53, 94

Daniel, Wayne, 125, 126
Danziger, Chris, 69, 70
Delhi Tests, 101, 128, 129
Denness, Mike, 71, 72, 80, 107–8, 109, 110, 114, 115–16, 118, 151
Dexter, Ted, 37, 65, 73
D'Oliveira, Basil, 92, 99
Duke of Norfolk's XI, tour of West Indies (1969–70), 75

Eastern Province, South Africa, 14–16
Edgbaston Test (1975), 115–16
Edmonds, Phil, 121
Edrich, John, 109, 111–12, 126, 149
Edwards, Ross, 120
Elliott, Charlie, 163
Engineer, Farokh, 92
English county cricket system, 105–7
Ensor, Paul, 35
Evans, David, 154, 159

Fag system (skunking), 47–9
Faulkner, Max, 86
Featherstone, Norman, 52
Fletcher, Keith, 71, 92, 101, 118, 130, 131
Francis, Bruce, 110

Gaekwad, A. D., 144
Gauhati, India, 130–31
Gavaskar, Sunil, 136, 144
Gillette Cup, 103
    1968 Final, 72–3
    1973 Final, 104–5
Gibbs, Lance, 125
Gilmour, Gary, 114
Gloucestershire, 70, 104–5
Golf, 32, 38–9
Gondolier café, Hove, 67
Gonski, Mr, neurologist, 11
Graves, Peter, 66, 93
Greenidge, Geoff, 103
Greig, Donna (née Reed: wife), 17, 34, 37, 74–80, 81, 94, 108, 122–3, 124, 152, 154, 165–6, 175
Greig, Ian (brother), 34–5, 47, 57, 61–2
Greig, Mrs Joyce (mother), 21, 22–4, 30–31, 32–3
Greig, Mark (son), 74, 78, 122, 175
Greig, Molly (sister), 34, 35–6, 74
Greig, Sally, see Hodson
Greig, Samantha (daughter), 17, 74, 78, 122, 157–8, 175
Greig, Sandy (father), 20–21, 23, 30–34, 39, 40, 44, 50, 53, 59–60, 69, 75, 91, 94, 167
Griffith, Billy, 72, 89
Griffith, Mike, 72, 103
Groote Schuur Hospital, Cape Town, 11

Hain, Peter, 86–7, 88
Hall, Wes, 125
Hampshire, 103
Hassett, Lindsay, 149
Headingley Tests (Leeds), 100, 121, 127
Higgs, Ken, 67
Hodson, Phil, 35
Hodson, Mrs Sally (née Greig: sister), 34, 35
Hogan, Paul, 160
Holding, Mike, 125–6

Hunte, Conrad, 59
Hutton, Len, 38, 149
Hutton, Richard, 77, 96

Illingworth, Ray, 76, 93, 94, 98, 99, 107, 108, 110, 116–17
India, MCC Tours of:
1972–3, 100–102, 107
1976–7, 101, 127–8, 129–48
Indian umpires, 127–8, 148
International Cricket Conference (ICC), 160
Iqbal, Asif, 103, 159

Jenner, Terry, 111
John Player League, 58, 106
Johnston, Brian, 149
Joshi, Uday, 103
J.P. Sport Pty Ltd, 160
Julien, Bernard, 103

Kallicharran, Alvin, 159–60
Kanhai, Rohan, 59, 92
Kei Mouth, South Africa, 22, 25
Kent, 103, 159
King, Rodney, 25–9, 84
Knott, Alan, 79–80, 92, 110, 118, 127, 131, 135, 153, 159, 170

Laker, Jim, 37, 99–100
Lal, Madan, 137
Lancashire, 67–8, 69
Larwood, Harold, 149
Lawry, Bill, 125
Ledden, Peter, 63–4, 66
Lenham, Les, 66
Levenson, Reuben, 65
Lever, John, 99, 128, 136, 138, 144
Lever, Peter, 93
Lewis, Tony, 101, 107, 117, 145
Lion Insurance Brokers, 174
Lillee, Dennis, 97, 98, 109–11, 112, 113, 114, 116, 119–20, 126, 148, 149, 150
Lindwall, R. R., 149
Lister, Jos, 121

miniature world tour of (1967–8), 70–71, 75
Lloyd, Clive, 92, 109
Long, Arnold, 164, 165
Lord, David, 160
Lord's Cricket Ground, 29
Greig's first visit to, 57–8
Jubilee Test (1977), 156
Long Room, 120
1972 Test, 99
1975 Test, 119–21
1976 Test, 125
see also Gillette Cup
Luckhurst, Brian, 98
Lynn, Vera, 39, 95

Madras Tests, 101, 142, 148
Maley, John, 169
Mansell, Alan, 94
Manzi, Teki ('Tackies'), 36–7, 83
Marsh, Rod, 111, 150–51
Marshall, Roger ('Bluey'), 104–5
Massie, Bob, 97–8, 99, 100
May, Peter, 37
MCC Schools, 52, 69
MCC Tours:
Australia (1970–1), 77, 93–4
Australia (1974–5), 79, 80, 109–14
Australia (1970–80), 168
Centenary Test Match, Australia (1977), 148, 150, 151, 163, 164
India (1972–3), 100–102, 107
India (1976–7), 101, 127–8, 129–48
New Zealand (1977–8), 161
Pakistan (1977–8), 161
provision for wives and families on, 79–80
South Africa (1964–5), 38, 108
Test fees for players, 168
West Indies (1967–8), 71
West Indies (1973–4), 107–9
McKenzie, Bob, 10
Melbourne Tests, 96–7, 114
Merrit, Andrew, 161

186

INDEX

Merwe, Peter van der, 52
Middlesex, 52, 165
Miller, K. R., 149
Mohammed, Sadiq, 105
Murray, Deryck, 125
National Service in South Africa, 53
Nawab of Pataudi, 65
Newlands cricket ground, Cape Town, 52
New Zealand, 151
  MCC Tour of (1977–78), 161
  see also Test Matches in England
Nomketa (Greig family servant), 36, 83
Northampton, 118–19
Nuffield Cricket Week, 51–2

Oakes, Jack, 44
Oakman, Alan, 57, 65, 66, 69
Old, Chris, 136, 144
Old Trafford Tests (Manchester), 97, 98–100, 126–7, 170
Oval Tests, 92–3, 122, 127

Packer, Kerry, 79, 117, 148, 158, 159, 160, 161, 166, 169–71, 172, 173, 175
  Greig signs contract with, 150–56
Pakistan, MCC tour of (1977–78), 161
  see also Test Matches in England
Parks, Jim, Jnr. 67, 72
Parks, Jim, Snr. 63–5
Passports, Greig's dual, 71–2
Pascoe, Len, 99
Patel, B. P., 144, 145, 146
Pendennis Castle, Greig travels to England on, 54, 55–6
Perth, 95, 110, 113, 149
Pollock, Graeme, 15, 16, 92
Pollock, Peter, 15, 16
Pope, Charlie, 10, 11
Port-of-Spain, 107, 109
Prasanna, E.A.S. 138, 141, 144, 145
Primary Club tie, 69
Procter, Mike, 50, 52, 87, 94, 105

Queen's College, 10, 57
  Greig's schooldays at, 40–50
  and coaching at, 41, 75
Queenstown, 31, 50, 83
  Greig's youth in, 20–22, 32–9, 40–54
  and marriage to Donna, 77, 94
Queenstown Golf Club, 32, 38–9
Queenstown Prep School, 43–4

Randall, Derek, 101, 132, 134, 135–6, 137, 138, 145, 150, 160
Reed, Donna see Greig, Donna
Rest of the World:
  Australian Tour (1970–71), 94–7
  England Tour (1970), 91–3
Rhodes, Dusty, umpire, 67
Rhodes, Harold, 71
Richards, Barry, 87, 92, 103, 149, 150
Richards, Viv, 106
Roberts, Andy, 103, 126
Robertson, Austin, 153, 160, 163
Rugby football, 46–7

St Andrew's College, Grahamstown, 77, 94
Scotland, 68, 75
  Greig's stay in, 34, 60, 70
Selborne College, East London, 45, 46
Sharma, P., 144, 145
Sheffield Shield, 123, 149
Shepherd, John, 103
Slade, Mr Justice, 161
Slynn, Mr Justice, 160
Smith, A. C., 73
Snow, John, 68, 92, 98–9, 100, 109, 120, 153
Sobers, Gary, 92, 94, 95, 96–8
Sobey, Vyv, 44
Solkar, Ekkie, 145
Sophie (Greig family cook), 36, 83
South Africa, 10–16, 81–90
  England tour of (1964–65), 38, 108

Greig's childhood and schooldays in, 20–54
and Christmas holidays, 61–2
and coaching, 75, 77, 94
Greig's views on apartheid and sport in, 81–8
South African Railways, 54–5
South African Schools, 46, 50, 52, 141
Sri Lanka, 148
Statham, Brian, 37, 67–8
Steele, David, 118–20, 121
Sugden, Richard, 29
Stewart, Mickey, 71
Subba-Row, Raman, 161
Sussex, 35, 63–73, 93, 103–5, 118–19, 159
  Gillette Cup Final (1968), 72–3
  Gillette Cup Final (1973), 104–5
  Greig joins club, 53, 55–60
  and first XI debut (1967), 66–8
  Greig appointed captain (1973), 102, 103–4
  and is suspended and leaves club (1977), 164–5
  Long Stop Bar, 65
Suttle, Ken, 57, 58, 66, 71
Switzerland, 75–6
Sydney, Australia, 114, 122–4, 125, 172
Sylvester, Malcolm, 63–5

Tackies see Manzi, Teki
Tayfield, Hughie, 141
Taylor, 'Dummy', 25
Test and County Cricket Board (TCCB), 160–62, 164, 172
Test Matches in England
  Australia (1972), 97–100
  Australia (1975), 28–9, 115–22
  Australia (1977), 156, 159
  India (1974), 109
  New Zealand (1973), 107
  Pakistan (1974), 109
  Rest of the World (1970), 91–3
  South Africa, 39
  West Indies (1973), 107

West Indies (1976), 124, 125–7
  see also MCC Tours
This Is Your Life (1977), 37, 167–8
Thomas, Bernard, 135, 139–40, 142–3
Thomson, Jeff, 110, 111–12, 113, 114, 116, 126, 159, 160
Titmus, Fred, 112
Tolchard, Roger, 132, 137, 138, 140–41
Trent Bridge, Nottingham, Tests at, 91–2, 100, 159
Trueman, Fred, 58
Turner, Alan, 120
Turner, Glenn, 128

Underwood, Derek, 71, 73, 100, 112, 131, 134, 136, 144, 153, 159, 167

Vaucluse, Sydney, Greig's home in, 74, 122
VFL Park, Melbourne, 168–9
Viswanath, G. R., 144
Voortman, Dr Sandy, 10–11, 12, 14
Wadekar, Ajit, 102
Walden-Smith, Audrey, 44
Walker, Max, 114, 116
Wanderers Ground, Johannesburg, 14
Warwickshire, 72–3
Waverley Club, Sydney, 122, 123
West Indian cricketers, 59
  Greig's remarks on BBC TV about, 89–90
  World Series Cricket and, 159–60
West Indies:
  Australian tour (1975–76), 122, 124–5
  Duke of Norfolk's XI's tour (1969–70), 75
  MCC Tour (1967–68), 71
  MCC Tour (1973–74), 107–9
  see also Test Matches in England

Western Australia, MCC 3–day
    match against, (1977), 149
Western Province team, 52
Williams, Col. P. C., 56
Willis, Bob, 99, 134, 136, 137,
    138–9, 142, 144–5, 156, 160
Woolmer, Bob, 132, 159, 160, 172

World Cup (1975), 115
World Series Cricket (WSC), 71,
    157, 158–62, 163, 164, 167,
    168–73

Yorkshire, 35